Grammar Rules!

Tanya Gibb

Australian Curriculum Edition

Name: ______________________________

Class: ______________________________

Grammar Rules! Student Book 1
Australian Curriculum Edition
ISBN: 978 0 6550 9249 0

Designer and typesetter: Trish Hayes
Illustrator: Stephen Michael King
Series editor: Marie James
Indigenous consultant: Al Fricker

Acknowledgement of Country
Matilda Education Australia acknowledges all Aboriginal and Torres Strait Islander Traditional Custodians of Country and recognises their continuing connection to land, sea, culture, and community. We pay our respects to Elders past and present.

This edition published in 2024 by **Matilda Education Australia**, an imprint of Meanwhile Education Pty
PO Box 118, Burwood, Victoria, Australia 3125
T: 1300 277 235
E: customersupport@matildaed.com.au
W: www.matildaeducation.com.au

First edition published in 2008 by Macmillan Science and Education Australia Pty Ltd

Publication data
Author: Tanya Gibb
Title: *Grammar Rules! Student Book 1 Australian Curriculum Edition*
ISBN: 978 0 6550 9249 0

A catalogue record for this book is available from the National Library of Australia

Printed in China by Central
Sep-23

Contents

Note to Teachers and Parents....4
Scope and Sequence....6
1 Things in the Garden....8
2 A Fish....10
3 A Family Tree....12
4 Our Weather Chart....14
5 Menu....16
6 Revision....18
7 Jobs on the Farm....20
8 At the Playground....22
9 Class Rules....24
10 A Fire Safety Visit....26
11 Goodbye Elvis....28
12 Revision....30
13 My Favourite Tree....32
14 Jokes....34
15 Our Favourite Pets....36
16 A Visit from Aunty Violet....38
17 How to Make an Under the Sea Diorama....40
18 Revision....42
19 Sleepy Cat....44
20 Dear Uncle Hugh and Uncle Kenan....46
21 When I Grow Up....48
22 The Lonely Dragon....50
23 How We Get Milk....52
24 Revision....54
25 Wednesday and Ruby....56
26 Buy Now!....58
27 Sharks....60
28 Cinderfella's Jobs....62
29 Magic Potion....64
30 Revision....66
31 Dingo and Wombat....68
32 How to Get Home....70
33 Book Review....72
34 Koalas....74
35 Revision....76
Glossary....78
Writing Log.... centre pull-out pages

Note to Teachers and Parents

Grammar Rules!

Grammar Rules! comprehensively supports implementation of the **Australian Curriculum English V9**, 2022, to develop 'students' knowledge and skills in listening, reading, viewing, speaking writing and creating'. The *Grammar Rules!* series is recursive and cumulative, with each year building on understandings developed in previous years.

The **Australian Curriculum English** recognises that knowledge and understanding of grammar at the level of the whole text and at the level of the sentence, clause, phrase or word, underpins students' comprehension of oral and written texts, and their ability to create effective texts for various purposes and audiences.

Grammar Rules! provides a conceptually sound, scope and sequence of context-based activities that support teaching and learning in English. Although the title for the series is *Grammar Rules!*, the series in not just about grammar. Each unit of work in the series begins at the level of the whole text by identifying purpose and audience for the model text, providing teaching opportunities to activate students' background knowledge of the topic or the text type, and then supporting students in reading comprehension. The texts provided can be used for discussion of text forms and features and sentence structures, as well as for vocabulary expansion. The texts can also be used as models for students to use when creating their own written, spoken or multimodal texts. The texts included in *Grammar Rules!* cover a variety of informative, imaginative and persuasive texts and hybrid texts that use elements of different types of texts.

Grammar Rules! also teaches the conventions of punctuation and some aspects of spelling (for example, plural nouns and homophones); literary elements such as onomatopoeia, rhyme and alliteration; and the way visual elements function to support or construct meaning. Other areas of the **Australian Curriculum English** covered in *Grammar Rules!* include critical reading and reflecting on character, setting and plot in narrative texts (literature).

Student Book 1

Units of work

Student Book 1 contains 35 weekly units of work presented in a conceptually sound scope and sequence. The intention is for students to work through the units in the sequence in which they are presented. See the **Scope and Sequence Chart** on pages 6–7 for more information. There are regular Revision Units that can be used for consolidation or assessment purposes.

The sample texts in *Student Book 1* are not tied to any particular content across other curriculum areas. This allows teachers and students to focus on the way language is structured in the different types of texts according to purpose and audience. Students can then use this knowledge to critically evaluate, respond to and create texts in other learning areas.

Icons

Encourages students to create texts of their own to demonstrate their understanding of the text structures and features taught in the unit. These activities focus on written language; however, many also provide opportunities for using spoken language to engage with others, make presentations and develop skills in using ICT.

Highlights useful grammatical rules and concepts. The rule is always introduced the first time students need it to complete an activity.

Tells students that a special hint is provided for an activity. It might be a tip about language features, or a reminder to look at a rule in a previous unit.

Encourages students to assess their progress across each unit.

Grammar Rules! Glossary

A valuable glossary is provided at the end of *Student Book 1*. Teachers and students can use this as a reference for terminology used in *Student Book 1*. Page references are also given for the point in the book where the rule or tip was first introduced, so that students can go back to that unit if they need more information or further revision of the concept.

Grammar Rules! Student Book 1 (ISBN 9780655092490) © Tanya Gibb

Pull-Out Writing Log

At the centre of *Student Book 1* is a practical pull-out Writing Log so that students can keep track of the texts they have created or attempted to create. The Writing Log also includes a handy reminder of the writing process, as well as a checklist of types of texts for students to try.

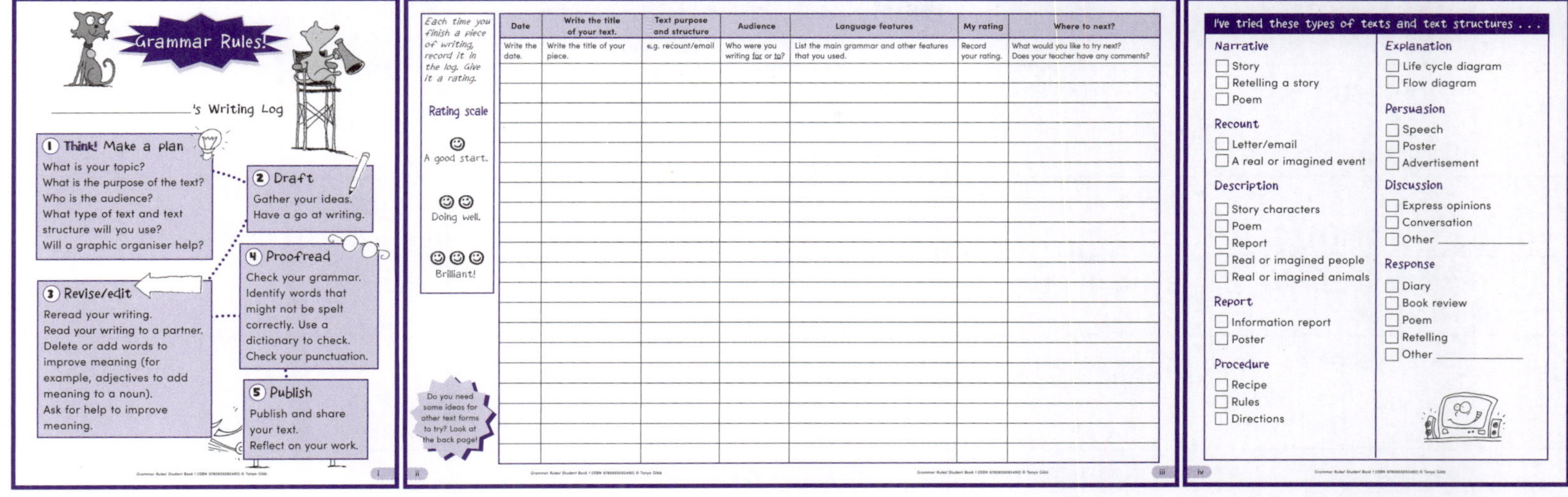

Grammar Rules!

_________________'s Writing Log

1 Think! Make a plan
What is your topic?
What is the purpose of the text?
Who is the audience?
What type of text and text structure will you use?
Will a graphic organiser help?

2 Draft
Gather your ideas.
Have a go at writing.

3 Revise/edit
Reread your writing.
Read your writing to a partner.
Delete or add words to improve meaning (for example, adjectives to add meaning to a noun).
Ask for help to improve meaning.

4 Proofread
Check your grammar.
Identify words that might not be spelt correctly. Use a dictionary to check.
Check your punctuation.

5 Publish
Publish and share your text.
Reflect on your work.

Each time you finish a piece of writing, record it in the log. Give it a rating.

Rating scale
☺ A good start.
☺☺ Doing well.
☺☺☺ Brilliant!

Date	Write the title of your text.	Text purpose and structure	Audience	Language features	My rating	Where to next?
Write the date.	Write the title of your piece.	e.g. recount/email	Who were you writing for or to?	List the main grammar and other features that you used.	Record your rating.	What would you like to try next? Does your teacher have any comments?

Do you need some ideas for other text forms to try? Look at the back page!

I've tried these types of texts and text structures . . .

Narrative
- ☐ Story
- ☐ Retelling a story
- ☐ Poem

Recount
- ☐ Letter/email
- ☐ A real or imagined event

Description
- ☐ Story characters
- ☐ Poem
- ☐ Report
- ☐ Real or imagined people
- ☐ Real or imagined animals

Report
- ☐ Information report
- ☐ Poster

Procedure
- ☐ Recipe
- ☐ Rules
- ☐ Directions

Explanation
- ☐ Life cycle diagram
- ☐ Flow diagram

Persuasion
- ☐ Speech
- ☐ Poster
- ☐ Advertisement

Discussion
- ☐ Express opinions
- ☐ Conversation
- ☐ Other ____________

Response
- ☐ Diary
- ☐ Book review
- ☐ Poem
- ☐ Retelling
- ☐ Other ____________

Unit at a glance

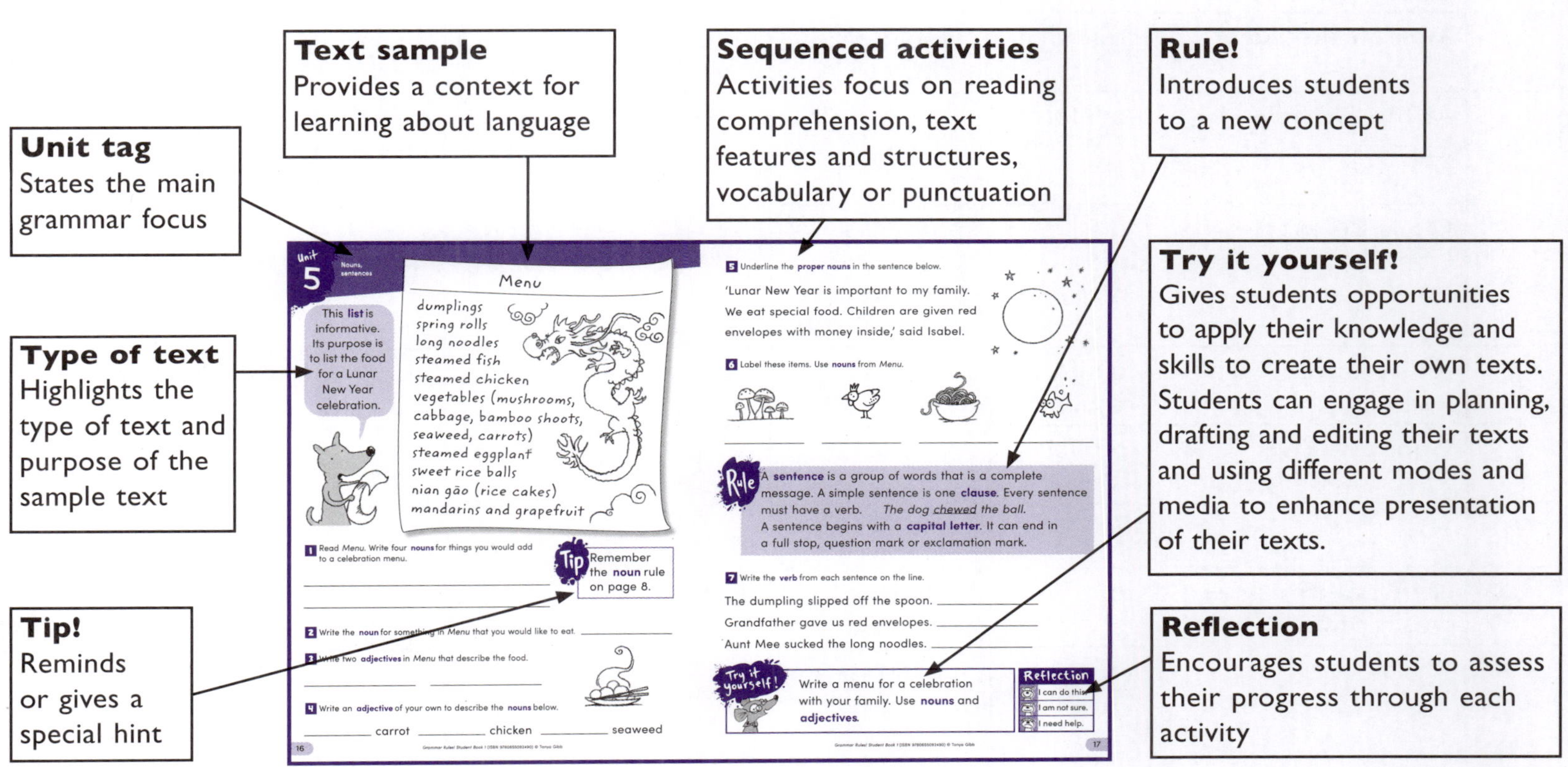

Grammar Rules! Teacher Resource Book 1–2

Full teacher support for *Student Book 1* is provided by *Grammar Rules! Teacher Resource Book 1–2*.

Here you will find valuable background information about teaching English, along with practical resources, such as:

- ☆ strategies for teaching text structures and features
- ☆ literacy games and activities
- ☆ assessment strategies
- ☆ grammar and punctuation wall charts
- ☆ teaching tips for every unit in *Student Book 1*
- ☆ answers for every unit in *Student Book 1*.

Scope and Sequence

This scope and sequence chart is based on the requirements of the Australian Curriculum English.

Unit	Unit name/ Type of text	Purpose of text	Clauses, sentences, conjunctions	Nouns, noun groups, pronouns, adjectives	Verbs	Adverbs and adverb groups/ phrases	Elements of language
1	**Things in the Garden** Diagram	to inform	sentences	common nouns	doing verbs		labels
2	**A Fish** Diagram	to inform	sentences	common nouns	doing verbs	phrases that tell where	labels
3	**A Family Tree** Diagram	to inform	sentences	proper nouns			labels
4	**Our Weather Chart** Diagram	to inform	sentences	proper nouns, adjectives			labels
5	**Menu** List	to inform	simple sentences	nouns, adjectives	doing verbs		
6	REVISION						
7	**Jobs on the Farm** Map	to inform	commands, sentences	adjectives	doing verbs		
8	**At the Playground** Recount	to inform			doing verbs	adverbs and phrases that tell when	opinions
9	**Class Rules** List	to inform/ instruct	sentences, commands, exclamations, conjunctions		doing verbs		
10	**A Fire Safety Visit** Recount	to inform/ respond	sentences			phrases that tell when	opinions
11	**Goodbye Elvis** Recount/Reflection	to inform		adjectives	saying verbs		opinions
12	REVISION						
13	**My Favourite Tree** Description	to inform	sentences, conjunctions	adjectives	being verbs		opinions
14	**Jokes**	to entertain	questions– open and closed, sentences				homophones, word play
15	**Our Favourite Pets** Graph	to inform	clauses, conjunctions, sentences	singular and plural nouns			labels
16	**A Visit from Aunty Violet** Report	to inform/ respond	sentences	adjectives			story characters, paragraphs
17	**How to Make an Under the Sea Diorama** Procedure	to inform/ instruct	commands	articles	doing verbs		
18	REVISION						

Unit	Unit name/ Type of text	Purpose of text	Clauses, sentences, conjunctions	Nouns, noun groups, pronouns, adjectives	Verbs	Adverbs and adverb groups/ phrases	Elements of language
19	**Sleepy Cat** Poem	to entertain		personal pronouns			rhyme
20	**Dear Uncle Hugh and Uncle Kenan** Personal response	to respond	sentences	proper nouns, adjectives			opinions and reasons
21	**When I Grow Up** Discussion	to inform/ give an opinion	clauses, conjunctions				opinions and reasons
22	**The Lonely Dragon** Narrative	to entertain	clauses, conjunctions				story characters, setting, plot
23	**How We Get Milk** Explanation	to inform/ explain	sentences				fact and opinion, labels
24	REVISION						
25	**Wednesday and Ruby** Narrative	to entertain	sentences	adjectives	verbs		onomatopoeia, story characters, paragraphs
26	**Buy Now!** Advertisement	to persuade		adjectives that compare			alliteration, opinion and reason
27	**Sharks** Argument	to persuade	sentences		thinking verbs		opinions and reasons
28	**Cinderfella's Jobs** List	to inform/ instruct	commands			adverbs that tell how	
29	**Magic Potion** Recipe	to entertain	commands	noun groups, adjectives			
30	REVISION						
31	**Dingo and Wombat** Narrative (fable)	to entertain/ teach a moral	conjunctions, word families				animal characters, plot, setting
32	**How to Get Home** Directions and map for imaginary place	to entertain	commands			adverbs and phrases that tell where	story characters
33	**Book Review** Response	to inform/ respond	sentences, questions	adjectives, noun groups	saying verbs		opinion and reason
34	**Koalas** Information report	to inform	clauses, sentences	pronouns, adjectives	being verbs, saying verbs	adverbs and phrases	paragraphs
35	REVISION						

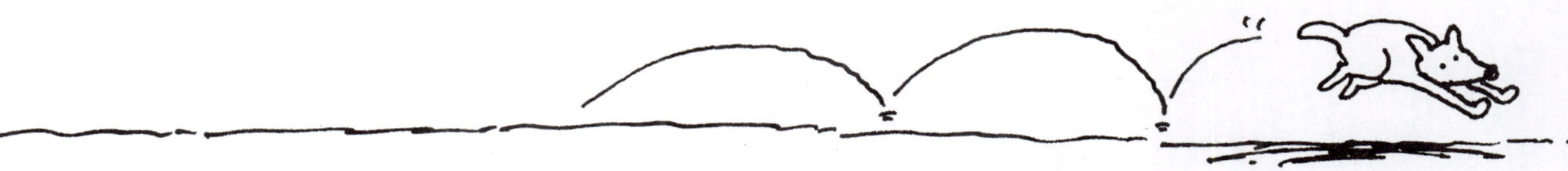

Unit 1 Common nouns, doing verbs

Things in the Garden

This **diagram** is informative. It shows things in a garden.

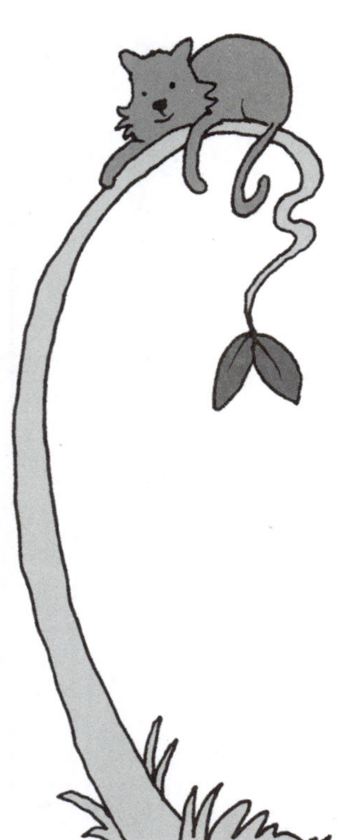

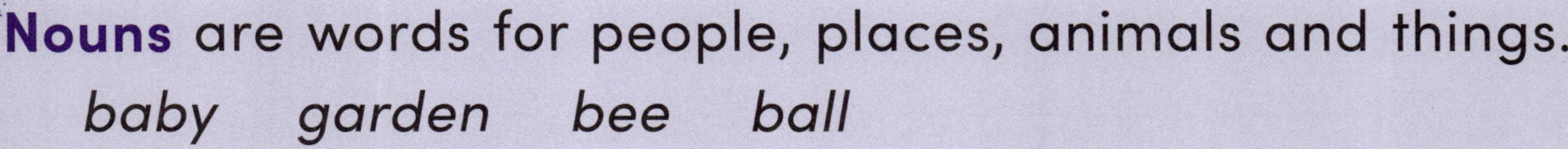

Rule **Nouns** are words for people, places, animals and things.

baby *garden* *bee* *ball*

1 Label the things in the diagram. Write these **nouns** in the boxes.

flower tree bird ball dog

fence bee grass nest frog

Grammar Rules! Student Book 1 (ISBN 9780655092490) © Tanya Gibb

Verbs tell what is happening in a sentence.
Doing verbs tell the actions.

jump *swings* *run* *swims* *hopped*

2 Choose the correct **verbs** from the box to complete the sentences.

flies
ran
rolls
swims
sits

A bird ______________ in the nest.

A frog ______________ in the pond.

A bee ______________ to the flower.

A ball ______________ on the grass.

My dog ______________ in the garden.

3 Circle the **doing verb** in each sentence.

Tom threw the ball onto the grass. It rolled beside a flower. The dog took it into the pond.

4 Read the story below. Circle the **verb** in each sentence.

The dog sat in the garden. A spaceship landed beside her. She ran to it. It flew away.

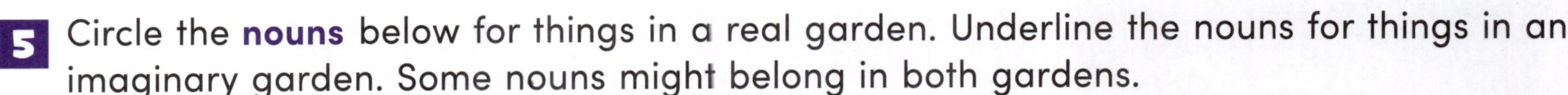

5 Circle the **nouns** below for things in a real garden. Underline the nouns for things in an imaginary garden. Some nouns might belong in both gardens.

beetle	elf	worm	flowers	butterfly	
fairy	ant	pond	grass	trees	nest

Draw a real or imaginary garden where you would like to play. Label your drawing. Use **nouns**.

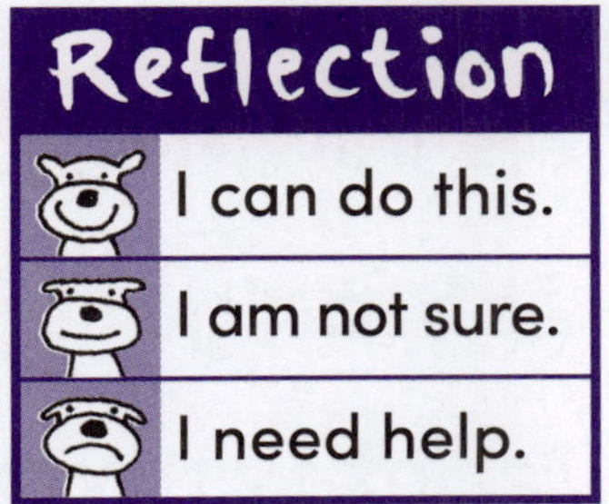

Unit 2

Phrases that tell where, nouns, doing verbs

This **diagram** is informative. It has labels to give information.

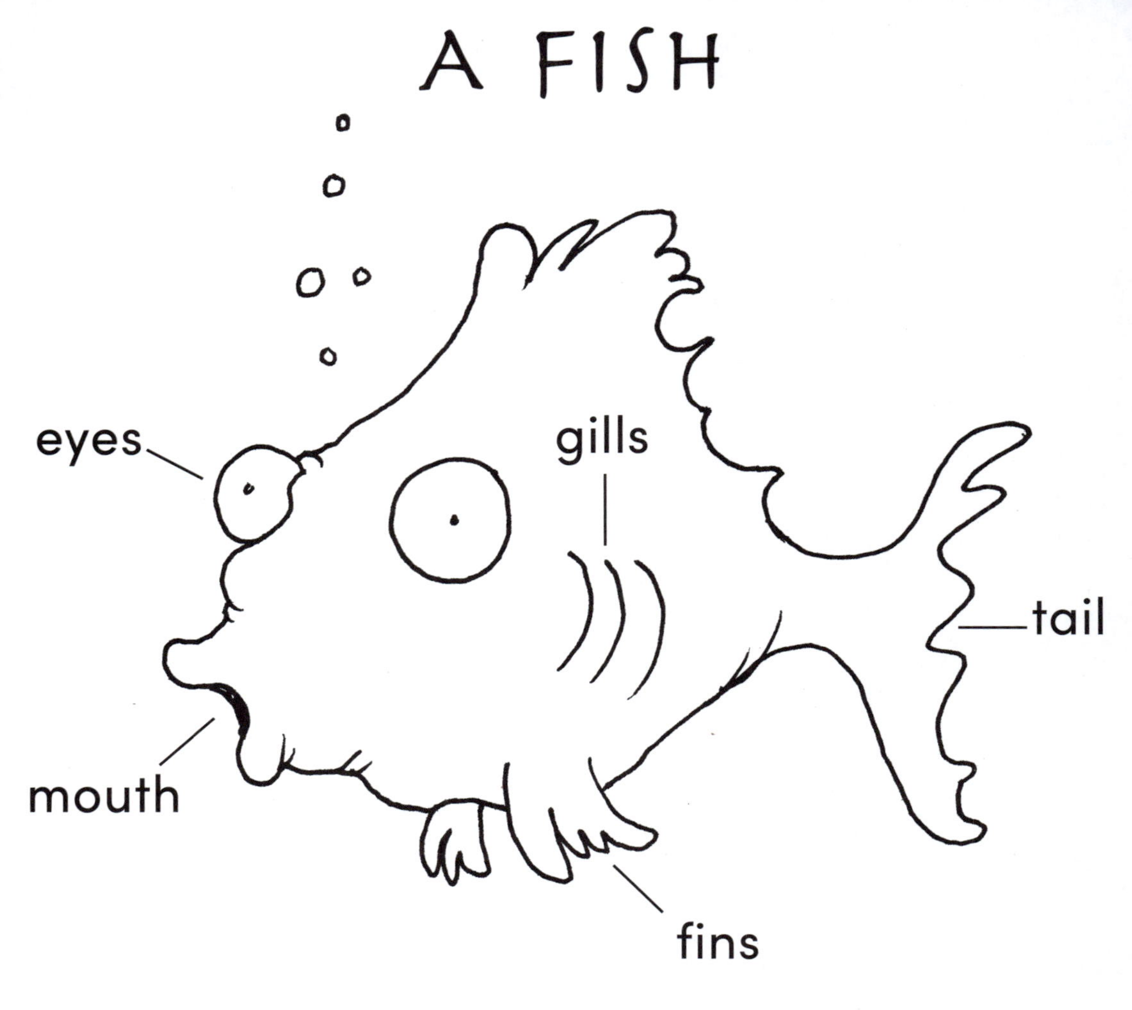

1 Look at the diagram of the fish. Write a **noun** from the diagram on each line.

This is a ____________. It has a ____________.

It has two ____________. It has ____________ and a ____________.

Phrases can tell where activities happen.

in the nest *under a tree* *on the grass*

2 Choose the correct **phrase** from the box to tell where.

on grasslands	in the sea	in the rainforest

Fish swim ________________________.

Zebras gallop ________________________.

Monkeys swing ________________________.

Grammar Rules! Student Book 1 (ISBN 9780655092490) © Tanya Gibb

3 Choose a **noun** from the box to label each animal.

dog	duck	koala	sheep

______________ ______________ ______________ ______________

4 Circle the **doing verbs** in the sentences below.

The kangaroo jumped across the grass.

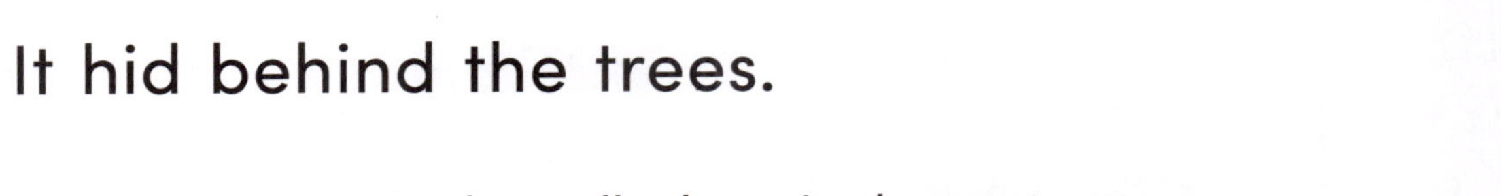

It hid behind the trees.

Write two **phrases** that tell <u>where</u> in the sentences.

____

____

5 Circle the **doing verbs** for things a real-life fish can do.

swim jump skip float swing eat look hop

6 Write about an animal and what it does. Use **doing verbs**.

____

____

Draw a real or imaginary animal. Label your drawing. Use **nouns**.

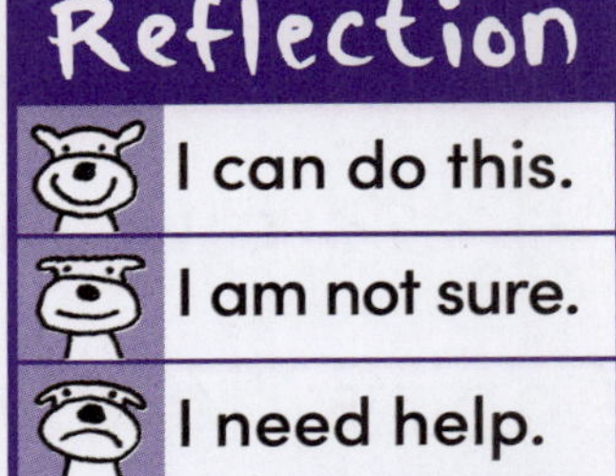

Reflection

- I can do this.
- I am not sure.
- I need help.

This **diagram** is informative. The writer's purpose is to show information about family members.

A Family Tree

People's names are **proper nouns**.
Proper nouns start with a **capital letter**.

1 Colour the circle for Anna in *A Family Tree*. Write the names of Anna's grandparents.

____________ ____________ ____________ ____________

2 Write a name from *A Family Tree* on each line.

Anna's mum is ____________. Anna's cat is ____________.

Anna's dad is ____________. Anna's brother is ____________.

3 Write your name.

____

Draw a picture of yourself.

Label your drawing.

____

4 Write the names of three friends.

____

____

____

5 Write your teacher's name.

____

Ms Fish

6 Read *A Family Tree*. Tick to answer True or False.

	True	False
Anna has a stepbrother.	______	______
Anna's stepbrother is Luca.	______	______
Eddie is Anna's father.	______	______
Nonno is a grandparent.	______	______
Anna is Luca's sister.	______	______
Luca is Anna's uncle.	______	______

Create your own family tree. Use photos or drawings. Label it. Use capital letters for **proper nouns.**

This **weather chart** is informative. Its purpose is to give information about the weather.

OUR WEATHER CHART

Monday

hot

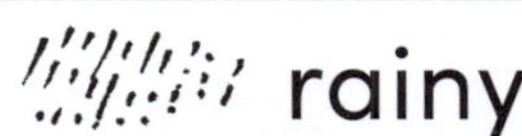
rainy

Tuesday

windy

cold

Thursday

cloudy

Friday

foggy

Today is Wednesday

The weather is sunny

We don't come to school on Saturday and Sunday.

Rule The days of the week and the months of the year are **proper nouns**. Proper nouns start with a **capital letter**.

March *Saturday* *Monday*

1 Look at *Our Weather Chart*. Write the days of the week in order.

__________ __________ __________ __________

__________ __________ __________

2 Choose words from *Our Weather Chart* to complete the simple sentences.

Today is ______________.

The weather is ______________.

Grammar Rules! Student Book 1 (ISBN 9780655092490) © Tanya Gibb

Adjectives tell more about **nouns**. They can describe.

sunny *happy* *black*

3 Write the seven **adjectives** from *Our Weather Chart*.

______ ______ ______ ______

______ ______ ______

4 Circle the **adjectives** in each sentence.

Wednesday was hot.

Friday will be sunny.

Monday was a busy day.

Sana had a happy day.

5 Write an **adjective** from *Our Weather Chart* on each line.

a ______ day

a ______ day

a ______ day

a ______ day

6 Fill in the missing letters. Circle the **nouns** for things you wear on a cold day.

j_mper

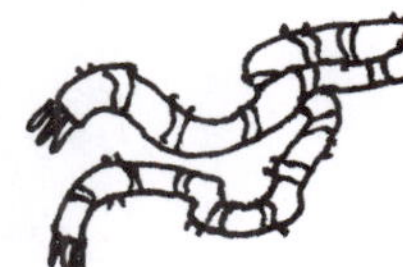

scar_

bean_e

swim__ers

t_ongs

jacke_

short_

Make a poster about weather. Add pictures and words. Tell about the things you can do. Use **adjectives**.

Reflection

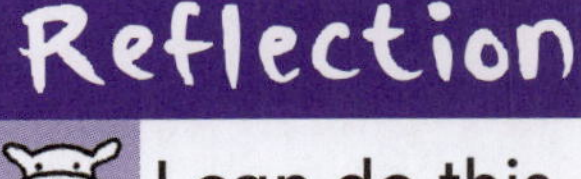

	I can do this.
	I am not sure.
	I need help.

This **list** is informative. Its purpose is to list the food for a Lunar New Year celebration.

Menu

dumplings
spring rolls
long noodles
steamed fish
steamed chicken
vegetables (mushrooms, cabbage, bamboo shoots, seaweed, carrots)
steamed eggplant
sweet rice balls
nian gāo (rice cakes)
mandarins and grapefruit

1 Read *Menu*. Write four **nouns** for things you would add to a celebration menu.

____

____

Remember the **noun** rule on page 8.

2 Write the **noun** for something in *Menu* that you would like to eat. ________________

3 Write two **adjectives** in *Menu* that describe the food.

____________________ ____________________

4 Write an **adjective** of your own to describe the **nouns** below.

____________ carrot ____________ chicken ____________ seaweed

5 Underline the **proper nouns** in the sentence below.

'Lunar New Year is important to my family. We eat special food. Children are given red envelopes with money inside,' said Isabel.

6 Label these items. Use **nouns** from *Menu*.

____________ ____________ ____________ ____________

Rule

A **sentence** is a group of words that is a complete message. A simple sentence is one **clause**. Every sentence must have a verb. *The dog chewed the ball.*

A sentence begins with a **capital letter**. It can end in a full stop, question mark or exclamation mark.

7 Write the **verb** from each sentence on the line.

The dumpling slipped off the spoon. ____________

Grandfather gave us red envelopes. ____________

Aunt Mee sucked the long noodles. ____________

Write a menu for a celebration with your family. Use **nouns** and **adjectives**.

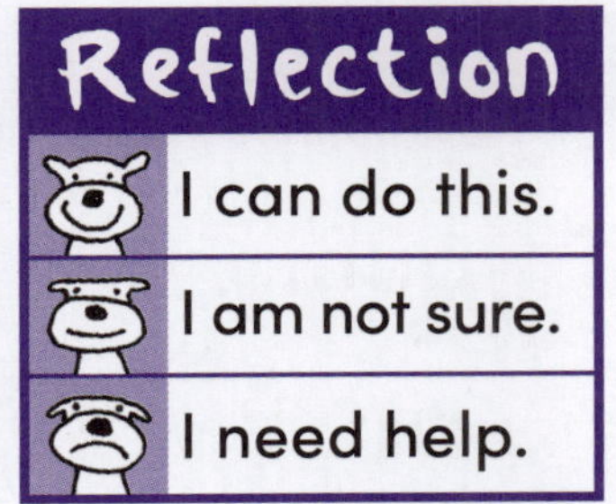

Unit 6
Revision

1 Write the **verb** from each sentence on the line.

The sunflower grew towards the sun. ______________

The bird flew to the nest. ______________

The frog jumped in the pond. ______________

Uncle Tomas chopped the eggplant. ______________

We ate rice cakes for Lunar New Year. ______________

The fish swam in the sea. ______________

2 Choose the correct **adjective** from the box. Write it on the line.

happy	sunny	big	pretty

The weather for the picnic is ______________.

A ______________ bird came to our picnic.

We ate our food on a ______________ rug.

Zippy was a ______________ dog at the picnic.

3 Draw a line to link each **noun** to a **proper noun**.

month	Fluffball
day	October
uncle	Abby
aunt	Fred
cat	Wednesday

Grammar Rules! Student Book 1 (ISBN 9780655092490) © Tanya Gibb

4 Write each sentence correctly.

the sheep's name is brittany

____

holly went to nassim's home on wednesday

____

the koala sat in the tree

____

5 Circle the **doing verbs** in the sentence below.

Maliki ran across the dirt and hid
behind the rocks. ('Maliki' is a Warlpiri word for 'dog'.)

Write the two **phrases** that tell where in the sentences.

____

____

6 Circle the **doing verbs** in the sentences below.

A small bird flew over our heads. It landed on the grass.

Write the two **phrases** that tell where in the sentences.

____

____

7 Write a sentence about someone in your family. Use **nouns** and **adjectives**.

____

____

Jobs on the Farm

This **diagram** is informative. Its purpose is to show where things are on a farm.

A **command** is a sentence that tells someone to do something. *Do your homework.*

1 Draw arrows on the diagram above to mark a route around the farm →→→. Follow these commands.

1. Start at the gate.
2. Feed the pigs.
3. Collect the eggs.
4. Say hello to the cow.
5. Give the dog some water.
6. Hug Mum.
7. Help Dad.

Grammar Rules! Student Book 1 (ISBN 9780655092490) © Tanya Gibb

2 Write the **verb** used in each simple sentence on the lines.

The cow stood quietly. ________________

The chicken pecked at the fence. ________________

A sheep ran across the grass. ________________

An apple fell from the tree. ________________

Paolo collected the apples. ________________

Phoebe fed the pigs. ________________

Dad pegged the washing on the line. ________________

3 Write an **adjective** before each noun.

______________ chicken

______________ cow

______________ pig

______________ horse

______________ sheep

4 Draw lines to link each **doing verb** with the rest of the sentence.

Swim	over the fence.
Jump	an apple.
Eat	across the paddock.
Gallop	some water.
Drink	in the river.

5 What would you do on a farm? Write two sentences.

____

____

Draw a diagram for your home. Mark a route from your front door to your bed. Write directions to your bed.

The writer of this text **recounts** events and gives an opinion about the events.

At the Playground

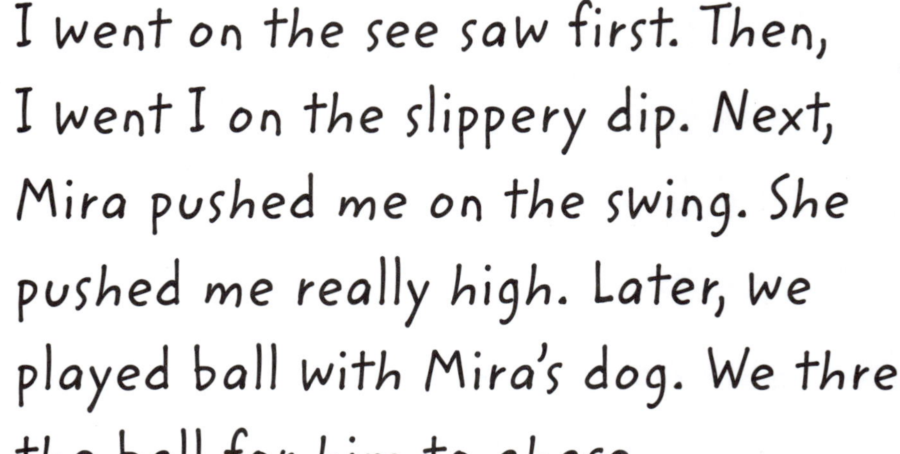

Mira took me to the playground after lunch.

I went on the see saw first. Then, I went I on the slippery dip. Next, Mira pushed me on the swing. She pushed me really high. Later, we played ball with Mira's dog. We threw the ball for him to chase.

I had great fun at the playground.

1 Read *At the Playground.* Underline the **nouns** for things in the playground.

2 Find two **phrases** that tell where in *At the Playground.* Write them on the line.

____

3 Choose the correct **doing verb** from the box. Write it on the line.

chased	threw	pushed	climbed	went

We ______________ to the playground.

I ______________ the slippery dip ladder.

Mira ______________ the swing.

We ______________ the ball.

Mira's dog ______________ the ball.

Grammar Rules! Student Book 1 (ISBN 9780655092490) © Tanya Gibb

Adverbs and **phrases** can tell when activities happen.

in the night *finally* *soon* *after lunch* *next*

4 Circle the **adverbs** and **phrases** that tell when in *At the Playground.*

5 Write words from the box on each line below.

Later	On Sunday	First

________________ Jamal and I went to the beach.

________________ we played on the sand. We built sandcastles.

________________ we went for a swim. The water was cold.

6 Circle the **verbs** for what a real dog can do.

eat write chase fly run read swim sleep scratch beg

7 Circle **doing verbs** that a hand can do.

throw write draw push sit read scratch see fly sneeze

8 Write sentences to tell what each animal is doing and where.

______________________________ ______________________________

______________________________ ______________________________

Try it yourself! Write a **recount** about somewhere you went. Use **adverbs** and **phrases** to tell where and when activities happened.

Reflection

- I can do this.
- I am not sure.
- I need help.

Unit 9

Commands, exclamations, conjunctions

These **rules** are informative. Their purpose is to tell children what to do in the classroom.

Class Rules

- ★ Work quietly.
- ★ Raise your hand to talk.
- ★ Listen to others.
- ★ Look after property.
- ★ Keep the classroom tidy.
- ★ Walk inside.
- ★ ______________________________
- ★ ______________________________

1 Read *Class Rules*. Each rule is a **command**. Underline the **doing verbs**.

2 Write two extra **commands** at the end of *Class Rules*.

3 Write a **command** that a family member gives you.

____

4 Write a **command** in each speech bubble.

Grammar Rules! Student Book 1 (ISBN 9780655092490) © Tanya Gibb

Rule

A **conjunction** (*and, but, or, so*) can join simple sentences to make a **compound sentence**.

Raise your hand to talk. Listen to others.

Raise your hand to talk <u>and</u> listen to others.

5 Underline the **conjunction** in this sentence.

Buy a fire extinguisher and learn how to use it.

6 Write a rule for your kitchen at home. Use a **conjunction** to write a compound sentence.

___

Rule

Some commands are **exclamations**. Exclamations are spoken loudly or in anger or surprise. They end in an **exclamation mark**.

Stop! *Look!* *No!*

★Have more fun!

7 Write an **exclamation** from the box on each line to show what you would shout at each event.

Stop!	Run!	Help!

A toddler is about to run onto the road. ______

You are going to fall out of a tree. ______

Your sister is playing soccer. ______

Write a set of **rules** for safety in the water or safety with an animal.

This informative text **recounts** events and gives an opinion about them.

A Fire Safety Visit

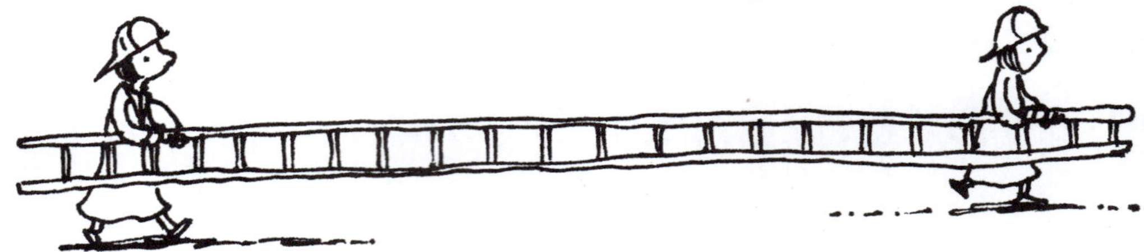

Firefighters visited our school today. First, they talked to us about fire safety in our homes. They said we all needed fire escape plans. Fire escape plans let everyone know what to do if there is a fire. Then they told us about smoke alarms. Finally, we took turns to sit in the fire engine. It was very exciting.

1 Read *A Fire Safety Visit*. Underline the four **adverbs** that tell when.

Remember the **adverbs** rule on page 23.

2 Draw a line to match each person to their role.

A firefighter	looks after your teeth.
A dentist	gives their time to help others.
An ambulance officer	helps to keep you safe.
A police officer	teaches you things.
An elder	cares for animals.
A vet	helps if you are hurt or sick.
A volunteer	prevents and puts out fires.

3 Copy the sentence in *A Fire Safety Visit* that gives the writer's opinion.

____

4 Write numbers 1 to 5 in the boxes to show the sequence in time.

☐ in the morning	☐ during lunch	☐ at bedtime
☐ after lunch	☐ before dinner	

5 Write the correct **phrase** on each line to tell <u>when</u>.

at night in the morning at sunset at sunrise in the afternoon

I eat breakfast ______________________.

I go to bed ______________________.

I get home from school ______________________.

The sun goes down ______________________.

The sun comes up ______________________.

6 Write a sentence for each **noun** below. Remember to use correct punctuation.

nurse	teacher	parent	coach

____

____

____

____

Write a **recount** about an event at school. Use **adverbs** and **phrases** to sequence events in time.

This **recount** is informative. The writer's purpose is to retell events and express their feelings.

Goodbye Elvis

My pet mouse became very sick on Friday. He did not move. He did not eat. He was very skinny and he had dull fur.

Mum and I took him to the vet. The vet told me that my mouse was dying. I did not want my mouse to suffer so I asked the vet to put him to sleep. I held him and the vet gave him a needle. He went to sleep and died very quickly.

It was very sad and I cried.

1 Read *Goodbye Elvis*. Write the **phrase** in the text that tells when the mouse became sick.

____

2 How does the writer of *Goodbye Elvis* feel? __________________

3 Circle the four **adjectives** in these sentences.

My mouse had dull grey fur. He was skinny.

He looked terrible.

Rule

Saying verbs tell that something is being said or has been said.

asked *told* *cried* *shouted* *said*

4 Circle the two **saying verbs** in *Goodbye Elvis*.

Grammar Rules! Student Book 1 (ISBN 9780655092490) © Tanya Gibb

5 Choose the correct **saying verb** from the box. Write it on the line.

gurgled
whispered
told
asked
giggled

Lauren ________________ at the clown.

Mum ________________ me to be quiet.

Dad ________________ for my help.

Nia ________________ in her stroller.

Chandra ________________ me a secret.

6 *'I love you,'* *said* *Mum.* Circle **saying verbs** you could use instead of *said*.

whispered chuckled giggled

barked **said** cried

yelled announced meowed

7 Draw a line to link each **saying verb** to an animal.

cheeped	chicken
clucked	horse
mooed	donkey
neighed	cow
brayed	bird

8 Write a **saying verb** from the box for each animal.

woofed	quacked
growled	snorted

The duck ________________.

The dog ________________.

The pig ________________.

The possum ________________.

Write a **recount**. Include things people have said. Use **saying verbs**.

Unit 12

Revision

1 In each speech bubble, write a **command** for the dog.

2 Write an **adverb** or **phrase** that tells <u>when</u> on each line.

'Can I do my homework ______

____________?' asked Riku.

'I want to watch TV __________

__________,' announced Daniil.

3 Draw a line to link each **noun** to a **doing verb**.

A shark	flies.
A kangaroo	swims.
A monkey	jumps.
A snake	swings.
A bird	slithers.

4 Circle the **conjunction** that joins the clauses in each sentence.

Cut the cake but don't eat the cake yet.

Wash the dog and she can dry off outside.

It's going to rain so take an umbrella.

5 Join the two sentences with a **conjunction**. Rewrite them as one sentence.

I think I will buy a book. I might buy a ball.

____

____

Grammar Rules! Student Book 1 (ISBN 9780655092490) © Tanya Gibb

6 Circle the **adjective** in each sentence.

The dog had big teeth.

Chen ate a crisp apple.

My sandwich was tasty.

We had a good time.

Ivy was feeling sick.

7 Circle the **verb** in each sentence.

My cat sleeps all day.

Alejandro ate a pie.

A kangaroo jumped past.

Misty chewed a shoe.

The storm knocked down the tree.

8 Write an **exclamation** from the box in each speech bubble.

Wow!	NO!	Hurrah!

9 Choose the correct **saying verb** from the box. Write it on the line.

ordered	asked	croaked	howled	laughed

'That was funny,' _______________ Dad.

'Do you think so?' _______________ Mum.

'Ribbipp,' _______________ the frog.

'Wooosh!' _______________ the wind.

'Clean your teeth,' _______________ the dentist.

Unit 13 Sentences, conjunctions, being verbs

My Favourite Tree

The tree in our school playground is a Moreton Bay fig tree. It has a thick trunk and thick branches. It is really old. It gives birds and insects a place to live. It gives us shade all year round. I eat my lunch under its canopy every day. It is a beautiful tree.

The writer's purpose is to describe the Moreton Bay fig tree and give an opinion about it.

1 Read *My Favourite Tree*. Write three reasons the writer likes the Moreton Bay fig tree.

___

___

___

Being verbs tell what things <u>are</u> or <u>have</u>.

It <u>is</u> sunny.   *I <u>am</u> hot.*   *I <u>have</u> a sun hat.*

2 Circle four **being verbs** in *My Favourite Tree*.

Grammar Rules! Student Book 1 (ISBN 9780655092490) © Tanya Gibb

3 Join the simple sentences. Use a **conjunction** to make a compound sentence. Write it on the line.

The tree is really big. I sit in its shade.

____

4 Draw a line to link the parts of the **sentences**.

Ben ate	the road.
Min held	the car.
Jade washed	my hand.
Ling crossed	two bananas.

5 Unjumble the **sentences**. Rewrite them correctly. Use **capital letters** and **full stops**.

dad pancakes cooked

____

brother my haircut got a

____

sat in the nest a bird

____

seagulls the dog chased

____

6 Add **full stops** where they are needed.

The tree is tall It has strong branches It is a gum tree

7 Draw a line to link the parts of each **command**.

Sit	your lunch.
Eat	away your lunch box.
Throw	under the tree.
Pack	your rubbish in the bin.

Remember the **command** rule on page 20.

8 Write a **command** to give your classmates.

____

Write a **description** of something at your school. Use **capital letters** and **full stops** in all your **sentences**.

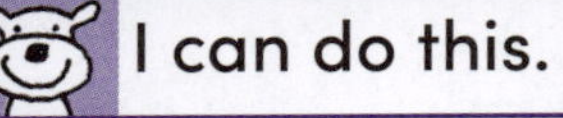 I can do this.

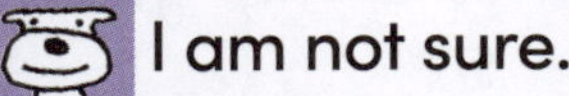 I am not sure.

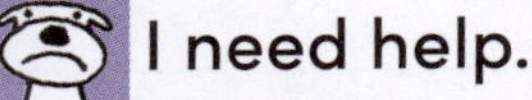 I need help.

Unit 14

Questions, word play, homophones

These jokes are imaginative. Their purpose is to entertain through word play.

Jokes

1. Question: What do moths study in school?
   Answer: Mothematics.

2. Question: Why is six afraid of seven?
   Answer: Because seven eight nine.

3. Knock Knock.
   Who's there?
   Boo.
   Boo who?
   Don't cry, it's only a joke.

Rule

A **question** is a sentence that asks something.
It ends in a **question mark**.
A closed question only needs a short answer.
Are you hungry?
An open question needs a more detailed answer.
What made the story so exciting?

1 Read the jokes to a friend. Underline the **question** in each joke.

2 Write a silly **question** you might ask a teacher.

___

Write a silly **question** you might ask a parent.

___

Grammar Rules! Student Book 1 (ISBN 9780655092490) © Tanya Gibb

A **homophone** is a word that sounds the same as another word but has a different meaning.

bear bare　　*pear pair pare*　　*to too two*

3 What is the homophone in *Jokes*? ______________________________

4 Write silly **questions** these people might ask.

5 Add a **question mark** or a **full stop** at the end of each sentence. Underline the open question.

I love pigs ☐

Where do you live ☐

Do pigs fly ☐

I live in Wellington ☐

Why do you love pigs ☐

Work with a group of friends. Collect riddles and other jokes with **questions**. Make a book of jokes.

Reflection

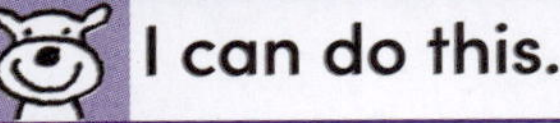

I can do this.

I am not sure.

I need help.

Unit 15

Singular and plural nouns, clauses, conjunctions

This **graph** is informative. Its purpose is to show the results of a vote.

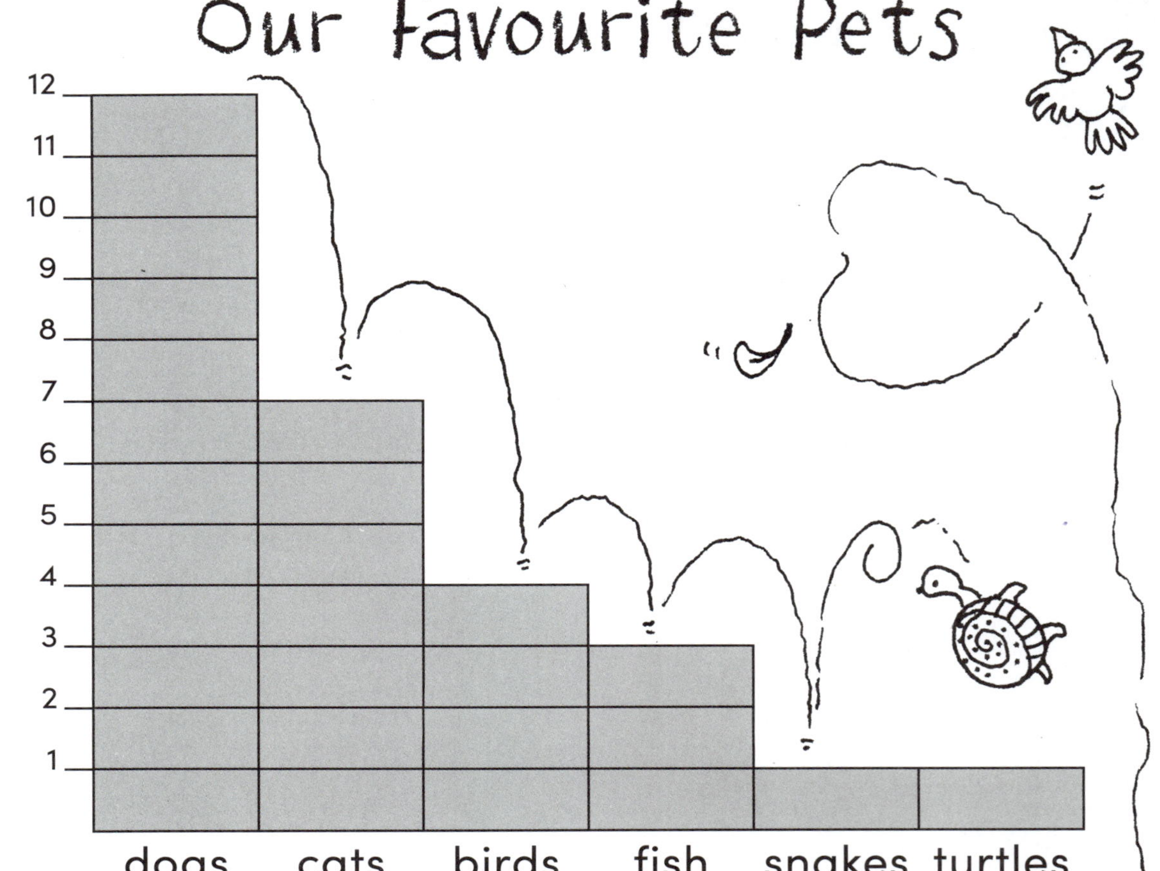

Our class voted on our favourite pets.
Twelve people think that dogs are the best pets.
Seven people think cats are best.
Four people like birds best.
Three people like fish best.
One person prefers snakes and one person prefers turtles.
So, dogs are the most popular pets for people in our class.

Rule

A **singular noun** names one person, place, animal or thing.
A **plural noun** names more than one. *hat → hats*

1 Read *Our Favourite Pets*. Now add **s** to make the **plural** for each **noun**.

one dog → two <u>dogs</u>

one cat → three ____________

one bird → four ____________

one snake → some ____________

one girl → many ____________

one boy → lots of ____________

Grammar Rules! Student Book 1 (ISBN 9780655092490) © Tanya Gibb

2 Add *es* to make the **plural** for each **noun**.

one sandwich → two sandwiches

one dress → three ________

one peach → four ________

one box → some ________

3 Write the **plural** for each **noun**.

one person → many people

one fish → lots of ________

one child → some ________

a fly → many ________

one loaf of bread → two ________ of bread

one tooth → all the ________

4 Label the pictures. Write a number and a **plural noun** or **singular noun**.

two pigs ________ ________ ________

5 Read *Our Favourite Pets*. Find the sentence that has two clauses joined by a **conjunction**. Write it on the lines.

____

____

6 What is your favourite kind of pet? ________________________

7 Finish the sentence.

If I had a pet dragon, I ________________________________

____

Ask your classmates to vote for their favourite pets. Make a **graph** to show how they voted.

Reflection

I can do this.

I am not sure.

I need help.

This is a **report**. The writer's purpose is to report to readers about a visitor to the school.

A Visit from Aunty Violet

We had an interesting visitor at school today. Her name was Aunty Violet.

Aunty Violet told us Dreaming stories and about her clan, the Gadigal people. Our school is on Gadigal country. Aunty Violet said that her ancestors had lived here for thousands of years before Captain Cook came here from England.

Aunty Violet is a good storyteller.

By Oliver

1 Read *A Visit from Aunty Violet.* Underline the **proper nouns**.

2 Find two **adjectives** in the text. Write them on the lines.

____

____

Tip Remember the **adjective** rule on page 15.

3 Circle the **verb** in each sentence.

'Budyeri kamaru,' said Aunty Violet. ''Budyeri kamaru' is 'hello' in the Gadigal language.'

4 Write a sentence from *A Visit from Aunty Violet* that lets you know that Oliver was happy about Aunty Violet's visit.

____

Rule

Characters in stories are described in specific ways to influence the way the reader feels about them.

Ethelred was always cranky. Bertram was sweet and kind.

5 Circle the **adjectives** below that would help to make the monster a likeable story character.

soft handsome cute

angry sweet

ugly kind

nasty funny

happy beautiful

6 In stories, there are many types of characters. Draw a line to link each **adjective** to a **noun** for a possible story character.

fierce	villain
brave	giraffe
curious	lion
sneaky	hero
evil	rat

7 Write as many **adjectives** as you can to describe a type of story character that you would NOT like.

Tip

Writers use words to make their writing interesting or more precise.

big → enormous, huge *good → deadly, fantastic*

8 Circle all the words that mean *small.*

tiny enormous little

great incy wincy

minuscule petite big

9 Circle the word used in *A Visit from Aunty Violet* that means 'tribe'.

gathering club clan

country friends

Write a **description** of an animal character for a story. Use **adjectives.**

Reflection

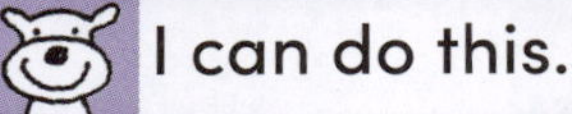 I can do this.

 I am not sure.

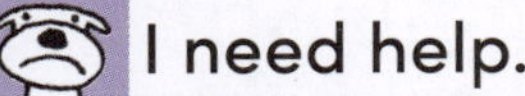 I need help.

Unit 17 Articles, commands

This text is informative. Its purpose is to instruct how to make a diorama.

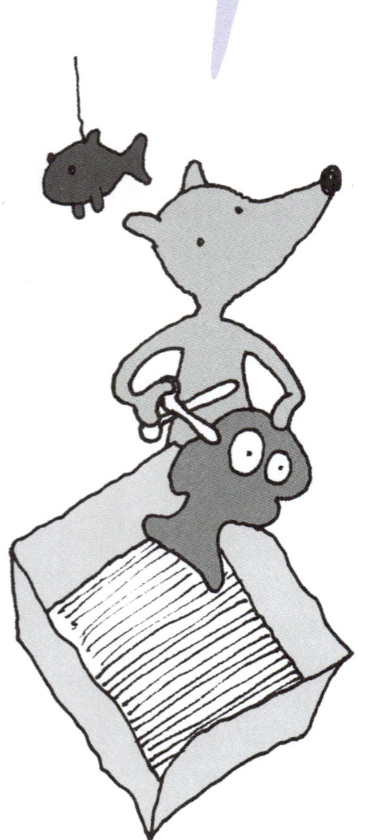

HOW TO MAKE AN UNDER THE SEA DIORAMA

What you need:

box
blue paint
felt-tip pens
scissors
coloured paper
cotton thread
tape
glue
rocks or pebbles

What to do:

1. Paint the inside of the box blue for the water.
2. Colour and cut out paper fish shapes.
3. Hang the fish inside the box on cotton thread.
4. Make coloured paper plants and reeds.
5. Place pebbles or rocks on the bottom of the box.

Instructions usually list equipment needed and what you have to do.

1 Read *How to Make an Under the Sea Diorama.* Circle the **doing verb** in each instruction.

2 Write five **nouns** used in *How to Make an Under the Sea Diorama.*

Grammar Rules!

________________'s Writing Log

1 Think! Make a plan

What is your topic?
What is the purpose of the text?
Who is the audience?
What type of text and text structure will you use?
Will a graphic organiser help?

2 Draft

Gather your ideas.
Have a go at writing.

3 Revise/edit

Reread your writing.
Read your writing to a partner.
Delete or add words to improve meaning (for example, adjectives to add meaning to a noun).
Ask for help to improve meaning.

4 Proofread

Check your grammar.
Identify words that might not be spelt correctly. Use a dictionary to check.
Check your punctuation.

5 Publish

Publish and share your text.
Reflect on your work.

Each time you finish a piece of writing, record it in the log. Give it a rating.

Rating scale

A good start.

Doing well.

Brilliant!

Date	Write the title of your text.	Text purpose and structure	Audience
Write the date.	Write the title of your piece.	e.g. recount/email	Who were you writing <u>for</u> or <u>to</u>

Do you need some ideas for other text forms to try? Look at the back page!

Grammar Rules! Student Book 1 (ISBN 9780655092490) © Tanya Gibb

Language features	My rating	Where to next?
ist the main grammar and other features hat you used.	Record your rating.	What would you like to try next? Does your teacher have any comments?

I've tried these types of texts and text structures . . .

Narrative

- [ ] Story
- [ ] Retelling a story
- [ ] Poem

Recount

- [ ] Letter/email
- [ ] A real or imagined event

Description

- [ ] Story characters
- [ ] Poem
- [ ] Report
- [ ] Real or imagined people
- [ ] Real or imagined animals

Report

- [ ] Information report
- [ ] Poster

Procedure

- [ ] Recipe
- [ ] Rules
- [ ] Directions

Explanation

- [ ] Life cycle diagram
- [ ] Flow diagram

Persuasion

- [ ] Speech
- [ ] Poster
- [ ] Advertisement

Discussion

- [ ] Express opinions
- [ ] Conversation
- [ ] Other ____________________

Response

- [ ] Diary
- [ ] Book review
- [ ] Poem
- [ ] Retelling
- [ ] Other ____________________

3 Draw lines to link the parts of each **command**.

Share	the ice-cream.
Peel	the chocolates.
Pour	the potatoes.
Lick	the watermelon.
Cut	the milk.

4 Complete each **command** for a dog. Use a **doing verb** from the box.

Roll Run Jump Chase Lie

__________ down.

__________ the ball.

__________ through the hoop.

__________ over.

__________ around the park.

Rule

Articles are *a, an, the*. Use *a* for words beginning with a consonant. Use *an* for words beginning with a vowel. Use *the* for a specific noun. *a box* *an eel* *the shark*

5 Write the correct **article** (*a, an, the*) on each line.

I cut ________ red fish carefully for my diorama.

I will make ________ wild animal diorama next week.

My next diorama will have ________ lion and ________ elephant.

6 Tick each sentence that is a **command**.

I love guinea pigs. ☐

Can you count to 100? ☐

Kiss me. ☐

Finish your dinner. ☐

Get a haircut. ☐

Where's Mum? ☐

Try it yourself!

Write a set of **instructions** for making something. Start each instruction with a **doing verb**.

Reflection

I can do this.

I am not sure.

I need help.

Unit
18 Revision

1 Write a **sentence** to answer each **question**.

What did you have for breakfast?

____

What is your favourite food?

____

2 Add a **full stop**, an **exclamation mark** or a **question mark** to the end of each sentence.

The gorilla would like some fruit ☐

Please feed the gorilla ☐

Look out for the spider ☐

Can you grow a moustache ☐

I cannot grow a moustache ☐

3 Write the correct **article** *(the, a, an)* on each line.

Rover, __________ dog, barks a lot.

Pass me __________ piece of cake with the strawberry on it.

I'll buy __________ banana from the tuck shop.

Charlotte wants __________ apple.

4 Write the **plural** for each **noun**.

one egg → two ______________

one tooth → three ______________

one flower → two ______________

one child → many ______________

Grammar Rules! Student Book 1 (ISBN 9780655092490) © Tanya Gibb

5 Follow the string to see what each animal is doing. Write the **sentences** on the lines.

The lion — is sleeping. ______________________

The bear — is eating. ______________________

The possum — is swimming. ______________________

The rat — is prowling. ______________________

The shark — is sneaking. ______________________

6 Write a **question** in each speech bubble.

7 *Mum was angry when I lost my school jumper.* Circle other words for *angry*.

peaceful furious happy mad cranky

pleased confused sad excited

8 Circle the **adjectives** that could describe a duck that is a story character.

quacked sky yellow sun

fluffy flower fly flew brave

bug lost angry talkative

Unit 19 Personal pronouns, rhyme

Sleepy Cat

Cleopatra is
a tabby cat.
We got her
at the pound.
She loves to sleep
on Daddy's lap.
Her tummy's
very round.

She sleeps
on brick walls
in the sun.
She sleeps
on Mummy's chair.
She sleeps and eats
and sleeps and purrs
and sleeps
just everywhere.

Rule **Personal pronouns** can be used in place of nouns.

me I we us you he him she her it they them

Ella and William are at the park. They will be home soon.

1 Read *Sleepy Cat*. Which two **personal pronouns** are used for Cleopatra? Underline them in the poem.

________________ ________________

2 Find the **personal pronoun** 'We' in *Sleepy Cat*. Who does 'We' mean?

____

3 What is a *pound* in the poem?

____

4 How does the poet want you to feel about Cleopatra? Write a sentence to answer.

____

Grammar Rules! Student Book 1 (ISBN 9780655092490) © Tanya Gibb

5 Choose the correct **personal pronoun** from the box. Write it on the line. If it begins a sentence use a **capital letter**.

she
I
her
they
he

_________ are coming to the concert.

Robert is missing. Where is _________?

Uncle Vince and _________ like lasagne.

_________ threw her shoe on the roof.

I like _________.

6 Write a **personal pronoun** on each line.

Bilal and Sienna went to the shop.

____________ bought bananas.

Bilal is going to make a banana cake.

____________ will take an hour to cook.

Rule **Rhyming** words have the same <u>end</u> sound.

hair pear bare where their

7 Find and write the two pairs of **rhyming** words in the poem. The rhyming words are at the ends of the lines.

________________ ________________

________________ ________________

8 Write six **rhyming** words for *sleep*.

____

Write a poem about an animal. Use **pronouns** in the place of nouns when it makes sense.

Reflection
I can do this.
I am not sure.
I need help.

Unit 20 Proper nouns

This is a letter. The writer's purpose is to **respond** to a holiday event.

Dear Uncle Hugh and Uncle Kenan,

I had a good time at your house during the holidays. Thank you for taking me to the aquarium. I liked the octopus, the sea star, the stingray and the shark. The most interesting thing at the aquarium was the shark egg. I didn't know that shark eggs look like big plastic corkscrews.

Love Lana

Mr Hugh Doyle and Mr Kenan Ceric
2 Hastings Road
Dharug Country
North Richmond
NSW 2754

Use **capital letters** for **proper nouns** for particular places and special days.

Kaurna Country *Naarm (Melbourne)* *Anzac Day*

1 Read *Dear Uncle Hugh and Uncle Kenan.* Underline three **proper nouns** for people's names.

2 Write the **proper noun** place names from the address on the envelope.

---

3 Write the **proper nouns** for your school's name.

Grammar Rules! Student Book 1 (ISBN 9780655092490) © Tanya Gibb

4 Write the **proper noun** or **proper nouns** for your town or suburb.

____

5 Rewrite the **proper nouns** correctly. Start each one with a **capital letter**.

australia ________________ mongo street ______________________

pookipoo public school ______________________________________

aunty tilly __________________ uncle bing ______________________

crazy kids child care centre __________________________________

arnhem land ______________________

6 Write your address on the envelope.

____

____

____

____

7 What did Lana say shark eggs look like?

____

____

8 Write three **adjectives** from Lana's letter to Uncle Hugh and Uncle Kenan.

____

____

____

9 Colour the **nouns** you might find at an aquarium.

elephant sea star octopus sea jelly koala stingray shark sheep

Try it yourself!

Write a **response** to something you have seen or a place you have been. Give your opinion about it.

Reflection

- I can do this.
- I am not sure.
- I need help.

Unit 21

Clauses, conjunctions

When I Grow Up

Some people in my class want to be pop stars when they grow up because they want to be rich and famous.

Other people in my class want to be police officers or firefighters because they want to help people and have adventures.

I want to be a teacher when I grow up because I want to be the boss and I like helping little children.

1 Read *When I Grow Up*. Circle the **personal pronouns**.

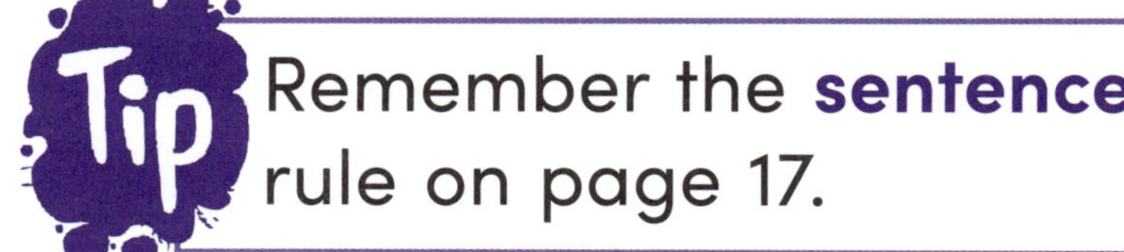

2 Circle the **sentences**.

Where jump

go shop glue

television shows

Sunglasses

I will buy a sandwich.

Follow the path.

chicken and mince

spaghetti bolognaise

Laura has a new watch.

Rule

Conjunctions (*but, because, although, unless, so, and, but, or*) can link clauses when giving opinions.

I love dolphins because they are very smart and they love their families.

3 Underline the **conjunctions** in *When I Grow Up*.

4 Draw lines to link each opinion with a reason or condition.

I hate washing our dog	because my friends are there.
I like choir practice	but only when it's very ripe.
I love pineapple	because she shakes water all over me.

Grammar Rules! Student Book 1 (ISBN 9780655092490) © Tanya Gibb

5 Write a **conjunction** from the box to join the clauses.

so	and	but	or	because	Although

Georgia wants to be a chef ______________ she loves cooking.

Nico hopes to be athlete ______________ he'd better get fit.

Leo loves spiders ______________ not redback spiders.

Hugo can skate ______________ Mulan can skate too.

Isla might be a truck driver ______________ she might join the army.

______________ she was tired, Evey could not sleep.

6 What job would you like to do when you grow up? Finish the sentence.

When I grow up I would like to be ______________________________

because ____.

7 Write your **opinions**.

My favourite television show is ______________________________

because ____

____

My favourite book is ______________________________________

because ____

____

Ask classmates what they want to be when they grow up. Write a **discussion** that gives their **opinions**.

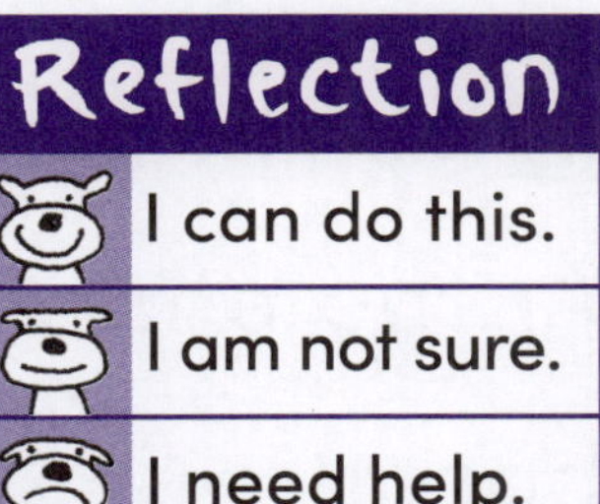

This **narrative** is about an imaginary character. It has an orientation, a complication and a resolution.

The Lonely Dragon

Once upon a time, on top of a mountain, in a land far, far away, there lived a dragon. She lived all alone because a knight had killed her parents. The dragon was sad and very lonely. She wanted a friend.

The dragon decided to leave her home and fly to the far corners of the earth to search for other dragons. She had many adventures but after a long, long time she finally found another sad and very lonely dragon. She was so excited.

The dragons flew together to her mountain-top home and they lived happily ever after.

1 When and where does the story begin?

____

2 How did the dragon feel at the beginning of the story? ______________________________

3 What did the dragon want? ______________________________

4 Complete this sentence.

At the end of the story, the dragon felt ______________________________

because ______________________________.

Grammar Rules! Student Book 1 (ISBN 9780655092490) © Tanya Gibb

5 Choose the correct **conjunctions** from the box to join the clauses.

and	so	because	but

The dragon left home ____________ she was lonely.

The dragon has a tail __________ she also has wings.

The dragon flew around the world ________ she could find a friend.

The dragon was friendly __________ she didn't have any friends.

6 Choose the best ending for each sentence. Write it on the line.

all the way to China.	happily ever after.
to the mountain top.	a friend.

The dragon flew ______________________________

In China the dragon found ______________________

Together the two dragons flew ___________________

They lived ___________________________________

7 Choose the correct **conjunctions** to join the clauses.

and so because but

I like snails ____________ I don't like slugs.

I like snails ____________ they leave a trail.

I eat crusts ____________ my hair will go curly.

The dog ate a snail ____________ it also ate a slug.

Write an adventure story. Describe the characters and the setting. What problem does the main character have?

Reflection

- I can do this.
- I am not sure.
- I need help.

Unit 23

Sentences, fact and opinion

This informative text is an **explanation** in the form of a flow diagram. It shows how we get milk.

How We Get Milk

Machines pump milk from the cow's udder.

Refrigerated trucks take the milk to the factory.

The milk is heated to kill any germs.

Then it is cooled again.

The milk is put in cartons and bottles.

Refrigerated trucks take the cartons and bottles to shops.

1 Read *How We Get Milk*. Now write numbers 1 to 6 in the boxes to show the sequence.

- ☐ The milk is cooled.
- ☐ The milk is bottled.
- ☐ The milk is heated.
- ☐ The milk goes to the factory.
- ☐ The milk goes to the shop.
- ☐ The milk is pumped out of the cow.

Grammar Rules! Student Book 1 (ISBN 9780655092490) © Tanya Gibb

Sentences make statements of **fact** or **opinion**.

My teacher is Mr Smart. *Mr Smart is fabulous.*

2 Write *fact* or *opinion* after each **sentence**.

Cows have udders. ____________ I like oat milk best. ____________

Cows make milk. ____________ Cows have four legs. ____________

Cows are cute. ____________ Baby cows drink milk. ____________

3 The sentences are muddled. Write them correctly. Use **capital letters** and **full stops**.

females are cows ________________________

are males bulls ________________________

calves baby cows called are ________________________

udders suck milk from calves ________________________

4 Write a word from the box on each line.

they milked drink milk

Cows are usually ____________ twice a day. On some farms ____________ are milked three times a day. Cows need to ____________ a lot of water to make ____________.

5 Write **rhyming** words.

cow ____________ ____________

day ____________ ____________

Tip: Remember the **rhyming** words rule on page 45.

Try it yourself! Work with a partner or in a group. Find out how we get a different food. Draw a flow diagram to explain the <u>sequence</u>. Label the diagram with facts.

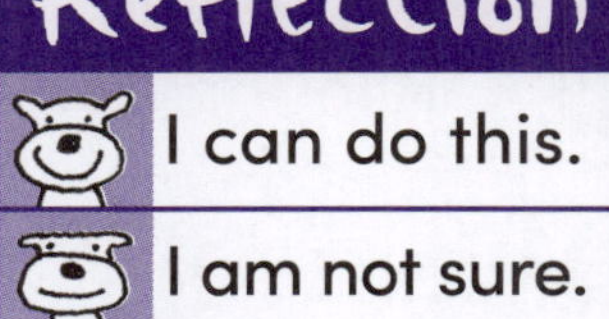

Reflection

I can do this.

I am not sure.

I need help.

Grammar Rules! Student Book 1 (ISBN 9780655092490) © Tanya Gibb

Unit 24 Revision

1 Write **rhyming** words.

sad ____________ ____________ sleep ____________ ____________

tent ____________ ____________ round ____________ ____________

2 Write the numbers 1 to 4 to show the sequence.

Watch the plant grow.	Plant a seed.	Water the seed.	Watch the flower grow.

☐	☐	☐	☐

3 Circle the words that let you know the pigs are happy.

Polly and Peter were excited to be outside in the sunshine. They loved to play.

How else can you tell the pigs are happy?

____

4 Choose the correct **personal pronoun** from the box. Write it on the line.

you they he she	
	Are Ted and Jenny coming? Yes ________ are.
	Will Nazeem come too? Yes ________ will.
	Will Leilani come too? Yes ________ will.
	Can I come? Yes ________ can.

5 Circle the **personal pronouns**.

go said you us me he she it

shop them they yell sink house

6 Rewrite each **sentence** correctly. Use **capital letters** and **full stops**.

yasmin lives in naarm, which is melbourne

____

eddie lives on baker street in mildura

____

aunty maggie lives in dunedoo

____

7 Write *fact* or *opinion* after each sentence.

Iceblocks are yummier than ice-creams. ____________

Magpies can fly. ____________ Emus can't fly. ____________

Dogs have ears. ____________ I love rainy days. ____________

8 Write a **fact** about something. ________________________

____

Write an **opinion** about something. Give a reason for your opinion. ____________

____

9 Use a **conjunction** from the box in each sentence to join the clauses.

and	so	but	because

I love Nan ____________ I love Pa.

I have ten fingers ____________ I only have two hands.

I brought my raincoat ____________ Mum thinks it's going to rain.

I brought my ball ____________ we can play soccer.

Unit 25

Onomatopoeia, adjectives

This imaginative text is part of a **narrative**. It introduces the main character and the character's problem.

Wednesday and Ruby

Once upon a time there was a puppy called Wednesday. She had a basket to sleep in, her own bowl to drink from, toys to play with and a human family to love her.

One day there was a huge storm. The wind howled. The rain thundered. The trees swished and swooshed. The branches smashed and crashed. Wednesday was scared.

Wednesday ran to get away from the storm. She ran and ran and by the time the storm was over she was lost. She began to cry. A sheep heard her cries.

The sheep said, "My name is Ruby. Don't cry. I will help you."

1 Read *Wednesday and Ruby*. The main character is ______________________.

2 Circle the **adjectives** that describe the puppy's home.

scary loving happy cold wet storm cry

uncomfortable comfortable loud basket sad

3 Why did Wednesday run?

____

Grammar Rules! Student Book 1 (ISBN 9780655092490) © Tanya Gibb

4 Add **verbs** from the story *Wednesday and Ruby* to complete the sentences.

The wind ______________.

The rain ______________.

The trees ______________ and ______________.

The branches ______________ and ______________.

5 Why did Wednesday cry?

____

6 Circle the **adjectives** that describe Ruby.

nice kind frightened caring mean funny

Rule

Onomatopoeia is when words sound like the thing they represent. *creak plop slurp*

creak

7 Write the correct **onomatopoeia** words on the lines.

Splat!	Snuffle thud!	Boom!	Chug chug chug!

__________! went the raindrops. __________! went the thunder.

__________ __________! went the possum in the roof.

__________ __________ __________! went the old steam train.

8 Write two **onomatopoeia** words of your own for the sounds of a storm.

______________ ______________

Try it yourself!

Write an ending (resolution) for the story, *Wednesday and Ruby*. Make sure to tell how the characters feel.

Reflection

I can do this.

I am not sure.

I need help.

Unit 26 Alliteration, adjectives that compare

This persuasive text is an advertisement. Its purpose is to persuade people to buy something.

1 Read *Buy Now!* What is the name of the drink in the advertisement?

____

2 Write the **adjective** in *Buy Now!* that says what colour the drink is. ______________

Write the **adjective** that says what the drink tastes like. ______________

3 Do you think you would like to try this drink? ______________

What might make someone want to try it?

____

What might make someone not want to try it?

____

Is *Buy Now!* selling to children or adults? ______________

Rule **Alliteration** is when the beginning of words sound the same.

smooth silky skin

4 Write the **alliteration** in *Buy Now!* S__________ S__________ S__________

Grammar Rules! Student Book 1 (ISBN 9780655092490) © Tanya Gibb

5 Write **proper nouns** on the lines to show **alliteration**.

Terrible T__________ tickled T__________ toes.

Lovely L __________ loves lemon lollies.

6 Write **adjectives** on the lines to show **alliteration**.

D__________ Dave draws d__________ dinosaurs.

S__________ Suri stole s__________ Sam's sneakers.

7 Circle the **personal pronouns** in *Buy Now!*

8 Write four **rhyming** words for *slime*.

__________ __________ __________ __________

Rule **Adjectives** can help when comparing things.

Lily is fast. *Housnia is faster.* *Charlotte is fastest.*

9 Use an **adjective** from the box to compare in each sentence.

better	softer	slower	hotter	best

I like chocolate smoothies __________ than Slime Shakes.

I like books about animals the __________ of all.

A possum is __________ than an echidna.

A snail is __________ than a spider.

Today is __________ than yesterday.

Try it yourself!

Make up a name for a new food. Create an advertisement to sell your new food.

Reflection

I can do this.

I am not sure.

I need help.

The writer's purpose is to give an opinion about sharks and try to convince others to accept their opinion.

Sharks

I think that sharks are really interesting animals. Some sharks, such as the grey nurse, are harmless to people. Some sharks, such as the great white, can be deadly to people. I believe that some people are unfair to sharks. They want to kill them just because they're sharks. They shouldn't hate sharks so much. People should protect sharks. The health of the ocean depends on sharks. I love sharks.

Rule

Thinking verbs are used for thoughts and feelings.

I feel happy. *I think it's cold.*

Ivy enjoyed the story. *Pippa dislikes cabbage.*

1 Read *Sharks*. Find and circle these **thinking verbs**: *think, believe.*

2 Circle the **thinking verb** in each sentence.

Tia remembered some shark facts.

I think sharks are interesting.

I love sharks.

Do you like sharks?

I hope people protect sharks.

3 Write **adjectives** from *Sharks* on the lines.

Sharks can be ______________ or ______________.

Grammar Rules! Student Book 1 (ISBN 9780655092490) © Tanya Gibb

4 Underline the writer's opening statement and concluding statement in *Sharks*.

5 Use **thinking verbs** from *Sharks* to complete the sentence.

The writer says that some people ______________ sharks and some people ______________ sharks.

6 What does the writer of *Sharks* want people to do about sharks?

____

7 Finish this sentence from *Sharks*.

The writer says that the health of the ocean

____

8 Which sharks are harmless to people?

____

9 Write four **adjectives** of your own to describe sharks.

____________ ____________ ____________ ____________

10 Write your **opinion** about sharks. Use *because* to give a reason for your opinion. Use **thinking verbs** for what you think and feel.

____

____

Work with a partner. Write a persuasive text. Tell readers that they should agree with your opinion and why. Use **thinking verbs**.

This text lists jobs for an imaginary story character, based on the fairy tale *Cinderella*.

Cinderfella's Jobs

1. Quietly clean the chimney.
2. Spotlessly mop the floors.
3. Briskly scrub the toilet.
4. Neatly make the beds.
5. Carefully wash the ball gowns.

1 Read *Cinderfella's Jobs*. Underline the **doing verb** in each **command**. Now circle a **noun** in each **command**.

2 Do you think Cinderfella needs to do the jobs in the sequence 1 to 5? Why or why not?

____

3 Which of *Cinderfella's Jobs* would you like least? Why?

____

4 If you had to do one of *Cinderfella's Jobs* which would you choose? Why?

____

____

Adverbs add meaning to verbs, other adverbs or adjectives. They can tell how to do something.

slowly *very quickly* *really quietly*

5 Write five **adverbs** from *Cinderfella's Jobs* that tell how. ____

____

Grammar Rules! Student Book 1 (ISBN 9780655092490) © Tanya Gibb

6 Use an **adverb** from the box in each sentence.

happily
slowly
kindly
badly
quickly
angrily

My brother sings ______________.

The dingo ran ______________.

The baby played ______________.

The turtle walked ______________.

The dog growled ______________.

The teacher smiled ______________.

La, la, la

7 Write an **adverb** from *Cinderfella's Jobs* on each line.

I ______________ tiptoed past the sleeping tiger.

I wrote the letter ______________.

I ______________ swept the path.

I ______________ tidied my room.

8 Write an **adverb** of your own on each line.

Pat the kitten ______________.

Wash the dog ______________.

Dad sings ______________ in the shower.

My sister chews ______________.

The baby sleeps ______________.

Aunty ate ______________.

Try it yourself!

Write a list of jobs for a story character, such as Goldilocks or one of the three little pigs.

Reflection

- I can do this.
- I am not sure.
- I need help.

Unit 29

Noun groups, adjectives

Magic Potion

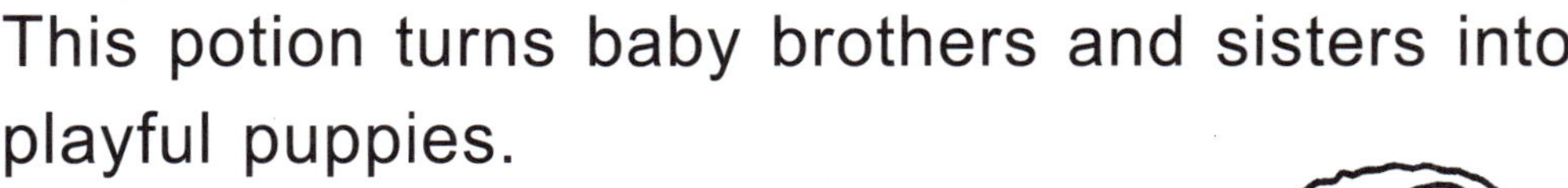

This potion turns baby brothers and sisters into playful puppies.

Ingredients:

- Two snail shells
- Three puppy hairs (any breed)
- 1/2 cup of goblin snot
- One nail clipping from the baby

Method:

1. Mix all ingredients in a small bowl.
2. Place one spoonful of the mixture on the baby's head.
3. Chant three times, "Playful, peaceful puppy!"
4. Be patient! The potion can take up to five minutes to work.

Warning: This potion only lasts for one hour. To make it stick for more than one hour, add some glue at Step 1.

This recipe is imaginative. Recipes use precise quantities.

Rule

A **noun group** is a group of words that includes a noun. A noun group can include an **article**, as well as **adjectives** that describe or tell quantity.

six squealing puppies baby brothers and sisters a few jobs

1 Circle the two **noun groups** in this sentence.

Mix all ingredients in a small bowl.

2 Would you like *Magic Potion* to be real? Why or why not?

___

___

Grammar Rules! Student Book 1 (ISBN 9780655092490) © Tanya Gibb

3 Choose the correct **adjective** from the box to complete the **noun groups**.

Many
Some
dozen
first

__________ children are away today.

__________ branches fell from the tree.

I ran in the __________ race.

Buy a __________ eggs.

4 Choose the correct **adjective** from the box to complete each **noun group**.

four
six
two
three
eight

A bird has __________ legs.

A horse has __________ legs.

An insect has __________ legs.

A spider has __________ legs.

Goldilocks annoyed the __________ bears.

5 Answer the questions about *Magic Potion*.

How long will the baby be a puppy? __________

How can the baby stay a puppy for longer? __________

What would happen if you could not find goblin snot?

____

6 Copy two examples of **alliteration** onto the lines.

____

____

Try it yourself!

Write a **recipe** for a magic potion. Use **noun groups**. Remember that recipes use precise quantities.

Reflection

- I can do this.
- I am not sure.
- I need help.

Unit

30 Revision

1 Use a **conjunction** from the box to join the **clauses**.

but	and	so	because

I think spiders are interesting ______________ they build webs.

I like gumbi gumbi jam _________ plum jam is better.

I love the book *Bindi* _________ I love the book *Somebody's Land*.

I hope we visit Uncle on Sunday _________ I can meet his new dog.

Happy Piggies

- Home for rescued pigs -

Cuddle and feed the pigs.

Wander through our gardens.

We promise you a great day out.

Visit soon!

2 Circle the correct answer or answers.

Happy Piggies is (imaginative/informative/persuasive).

3 What does the writer of *Happy Piggies* want you to do?

____

4 Write an **adverb** from the box on each line.

sadly
madly
happily
noisily
swiftly

Her eyebrows wiggled ______________.

The movie ended ______________.

The teacher smiled ______________.

The bird flew ______________.

The giant thumped ______________.

Grammar Rules! Student Book 1 (ISBN 9780655092490) © Tanya Gibb

5 Draw lines to link the rhyming words.

tree	stack
hose	speech
head	pear
time	rhyme
peach	shed
chair	flea
back	toes

6 Draw lines to link pairs of opposites.

right	down
tall	little
up	short
give	last
finish	start
big	take
first	wrong

7 Write a **thinking verb** from the box on each line.

enjoy	loved	think	like	understand

Did you ________________ your dinner?

I ________________ that story!

Would you ________________ some more ice-cream?

What do you ________________ about sharks?

Do you ________________ the Yugambeh language?

8 Choose the correct **adjective** to complete each noun group.

one	four	two	many	some

Strong zebras have ____________ legs.

Some camels have ____________ humps.

A hive has ____________ worker bees.

I'd like ____________ chocolate chip ice-cream.

A whale has ____________ huge tail.

This narrative is based on the fable *The Hare and the Tortoise*. It has an orientation, a complication and a resolution.

Dingo and Wombat

Once upon a time there was a dingo and a wombat.

One day, Dingo was teasing Wombat for being slow, so Wombat said, 'Let's race.' Dingo agreed, of course.

Kookaburra shouted, 'Go!' to start the race.

Dingo raced ahead. She thought she would easily win so she stopped to take a nap.

Wombat kept walking, slowly and steadily, and won the race.

The moral is 'slow and steady will win in the end'.

1 In stories like *Dingo and Wombat* the animal characters talk.

What might Wombat have said to Dingo before the race?

____

What might Dingo have said to Wombat after the race?

____

What might Wombat have said to Dingo after the race?

____

What might Kookaburra have said during the race?

____

Grammar Rules! Student Book 1 (ISBN 9780655092490) © Tanya Gibb

2 Use a **conjunction** from the box to join the **clauses**.

but	because	and	until

Wombat was slow ____________ she won the race.

Dingo was winning ____________ she stopped to take a nap.

Wombat was slow ____________ she was steady.

Wombat won ____________ Dingo stopped for a nap.

3 Circle the correct **adjective** in each sentence.

Wombat is smart / smarter than Dingo.

Dingo is faster / fast than Wombat.

Tip A **word family** is a group of words that has the same base word.

play *plays* *playing* *played* *playground*

4 Build **word families** for each word below.

race ________________________________

easy ________________________________

walk ________________________________

slow ________________________________

5 Where does *Dingo and Wombat* take place?

____

Try it yourself! Find an Aboriginal or Torres Strait Islander story that has animal characters. Read the story and then retell it to a partner.

This is an imaginative text. The **directions** help a story character find the way home.

HOW TO GET HOME

- Start at X.
- Walk along the path.
- Go across the bridge. (Beware of the troll under the bridge).
- Turn left at the fork in the path.
- Walk past the gingerbread house.
- Go around the tree. (Don't talk to the wolf behind the tree.)
- Keep walking along the path.
- Stop to help get the cat out of the well.
- Follow the path all the way to the cottage of the bears.

1 Help the Little Bear get home! Follow the **directions** above. Draw the route for the Little Bear on the map. Use arrows. → → →

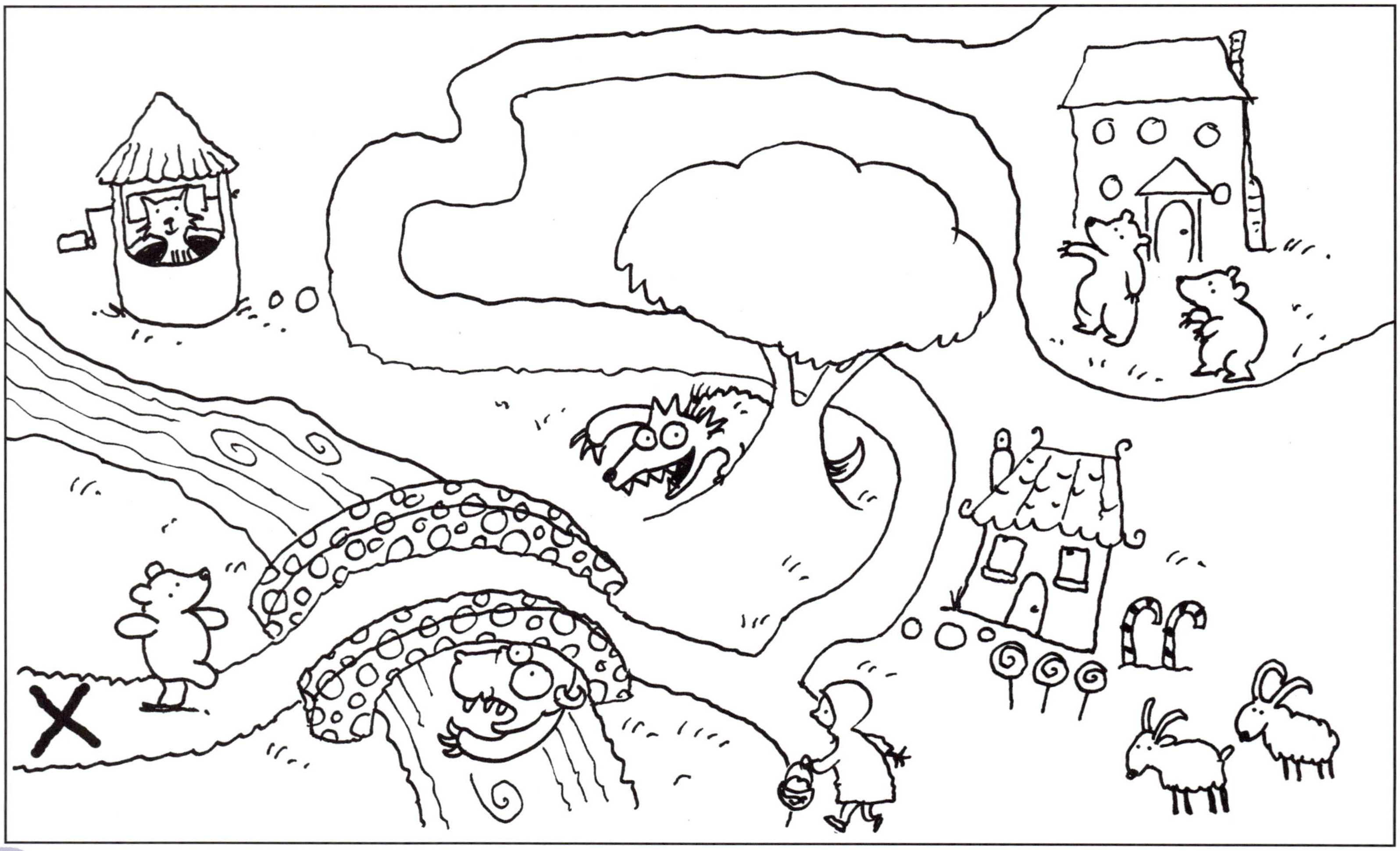

X

2 Write the two warnings in *How to Get Home.*

____

____

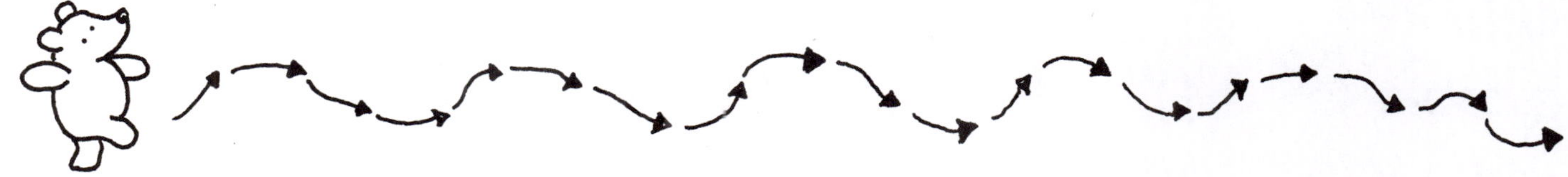

3 Write six **doing verbs** used in *How to Get Home.*

____

4 Underline four **phrases** that tell where in *How to Get Home.*

5 Write an **adverb** or **phrase** that tells where on each line. Use the map in question 1 to get ideas.

The bears waited ______________________________.

The wolf hid ______________________________.

The troll hid ______________________________.

The goats walked ______________________________.

Red Riding Hood strolled ______________________________.

6 Write an **adverb** or **phrase** that tells where for these things in your classroom.

Paint is kept ______________________________.

Books are stored ______________________________.

The teacher's desk is ______________________________.

The children sit ______________________________.

Draw a map for a story you have written or read. Write directions to tell a story character where to go.

Unit 33

Noun groups, saying verbs, opinions and reasons

The writer's purpose is to respond to a book she has read. She gives her opinion and reasons.

Book Review

Student's Name: Lilly

Title: The Bunyip of Berkeley's Creek

Author: Jenny Wagner

Illustrator: Ron Brooks

Comment: At first I thought the story was really sad.

The bunyip kept asking, 'What am I?' and all the animals said he was a horrible-looking bunyip. The bunyip sighed a long, deep sigh and went back to his waterhole.

But then another bunyip crawled out of the waterhole and asked, 'What am I?'

The bunyip yelled, 'You're a bunyip just like me!'

The story had a happy ending because the bunyip had found a friend. I really loved this story.

1 Read *Book Review*. Underline the **noun group** used by the animals to describe the bunyip.

2 What **noun group** might the bunyip use to describe the other bunyip?

---

3 Write the **question** that the bunyips asked.

---

4 Write the **noun group** that describes the bunyip's sigh in *Book Review*.

____

5 Write the sentence that tells Lilly's **opinion** of the book.

____

6 Does Lilly's *Book Review* persuade <u>you</u> to want to read the book? Why or why not?

____

7 How might the bunyip have felt when he yelled, 'You're a bunyip just like me!'?

____

8 Underline the **saying verbs**. Circle the **proper nouns**.

'I don't believe in bunyips,' said Sebastian.

'They are only in stories,' commented Mum.

'I love stories about bunyips,' replied Sophie.

'Me too,' agreed Sebastian.

9 Add a **verb** of your own to each line.

'I __________ sad for the bunyip,' __________ Lilly.

The bunyip __________ a long sigh.

'You __________ a bunyip,' __________ the bunyip.

Lilly __________ the story.

Write a book review about a book you like or dislike. Use **noun groups** that describe. Give your **opinions**.

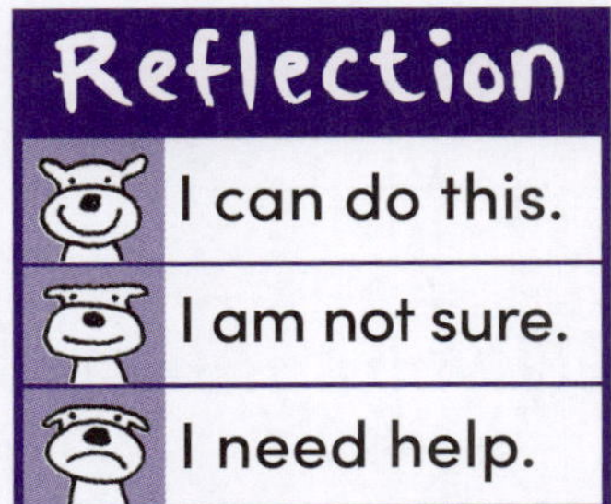

Unit 34

Verbs, pronouns

Koalas

Koalas are marsupials. Females have pouches for their babies.

Koalas have thick grey woolly fur. They live in trees and are excellent climbers. They eat eucalyptus leaves. Koalas sleep for 18 to 20 hours a day. They are most active at night.

Male koalas grunt and bellow. Female koalas bellow too, but they also make special sounds for their babies. Females murmur, hum and click. A frightened koala screams like a human baby.

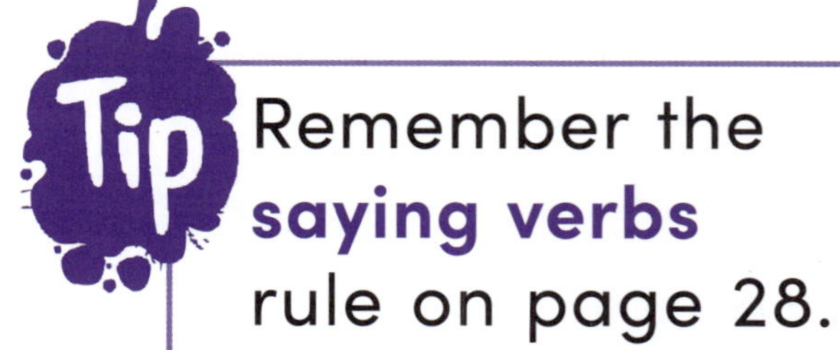

Tip: Remember the **saying verbs** rule on page 28.

1 Read *Koalas*. Underline all the **verbs**.

2 Write six **saying verbs** used in *Koalas*.

____

3 Write three **adjectives** used to describe a koala's fur.

______________ ______________ ______________

4 Write the **adjective** that describes a koala's ability to climb. ______________

Grammar Rules! Student Book 1 (ISBN 9780655092490) © Tanya Gibb

Repeating important words helps a text make sense.

5 In *Koalas*, circle the word *koalas*. How many times is it **repeated**? ________

6 Use a different colour and circle the **pronoun** *they*. How many times is it **repeated**? ________

7 Which noun does *they* replace in *Koalas*? ________________

8 Count the **being verbs** in *Koalas*. How many are there? __________

9 What does *marsupial* mean? Use a dictionary or ask an adult.

____

10 Why might a koala scream?

____

11 What information can be found in *Koalas*? Circle the answers.

what koalas are what koalas look like

what koalas do what the writer thinks about koalas

how the writer feels about koalas where koalas live

what koalas eat what koalas sound like

a koala's problems in the wild what hurts koalas

12 Write a **phrase** that tells <u>where</u> or <u>when</u> on each line.

Koalas live ________________.

They are most active ____________________.

Write an **information report** about an animal. **Repeat** the noun for your animal or use **pronouns** to replace the noun. Make sure the report makes sense.

Unit

35 Revision

1 Circle the **noun groups** in the sentences.

Aunty Liz bought a new bright red scarf.

Dom made a big mess.

Sasha has nice, friendly neighbours.

I saw six tiny, black and white puppies.

We live in a two-bedroom unit.

2 Write a **word family** for each word.

sleep ______________________________

play ______________________________

3 Add an **adverb** or **phrase** to each sentence to tell where or when.

The bunyip jumped ________________.

Rina will see the dentist ________________.

Henry threw the ball ________________.

4 Circle the **verbs** in the sentence.

The bunyip sighed and went back to the waterhole.

5 Write an **adjective** to describe each **noun**.

______________ koala ______________ baby

______________ tree ______________ dad

______________ mum ______________ principal

______________ friend ______________ playground

Grammar Rules! Student Book 1 (ISBN 9780655092490) © Tanya Gibb

6 Rewrite the words in the correct order to make sentences. Punctuate the sentences correctly.

school bag had to unpack mila her

____

live in penrith went to sara

____

shop went to the timmy apples to buy

____

7 Write words from the box on the lines.

babies Koalas They make eat trees sleep Female koala

Koalas are marsupials. _________ have thick, grey, woolly fur. _________ live in _________. Koalas _________ for 18 to 20 hours every day. Koalas only _________ eucalyptus leaves. Koalas _________ interesting noises. _________ koalas murmur and hum for their _________. A frightened _________ will scream.

8 Choose the correct **conjunction** from the box. Write it on the line.

and but so because

Goldilocks tried Daddy Bear's porridge _________ it was too hot.

Goldilocks tried Mummy Bear's bed _________ she tried Daddy Bear's bed.

Goldilocks ran _________ the bears were coming home.

Baby Bear's chair was broken _________ Mummy Bear fixed it.

Glossary

Look at the page number in the circle to find more information about the rule or tip.

adjective ..... a word that tells more about a **noun** 15
can compare 59

adverb/adverb group (includes prepositional phrases) ..... can tell where 10
can tell when 23
can tell how 62

alliteration ..... when the beginnings of words sound the same 58

article ..... a small word (*a, an, the*) used in front of a **noun** or at the start of a **noun group** 41

character ..... who a story is about. Characters are described in specific ways to influence how the reader feels about them. 39

clause ..... a group of words that includes a **verb**.
A simple sentence is one clause. 17

command ..... a sentence that tells someone to do something 20

compound sentence ..... a sentence that has two equal **clauses** joined by a **conjunction** 25

conjunction ..... a word that joins **clauses**, for example to link an opinion with a reason 25 48

exclamation ..... a sentence that shows strong emotion, like anger or surprise 25

homophone ..... a word that sounds the same as another word but has a different meaning 35

noun ..... a word for a person, place, animal or thing 8

common noun 8

proper noun 12 14 46

singular and plural 36

Grammar Rules! Student Book 1 (ISBN 9780655092490) © Tanya Gibb

noun group .... a group of words that includes a **noun** and other words that tell more about the noun 64

onomatopoeia .... when words sound like the things they represent 57

personal pronoun .... a word that is used in the place of a **noun** 44

phrase .... a group of words that does not include a **verb**; can do the job of an **adverb** to tell where (place), when (time) or how (manner) 10 23

question .... a sentence that asks something.
Questions can be open or closed. 34

rhyme .... when the ends of words sound the same 45

sentence .... a group of words that make a complete message
A sentence must include at least one **verb**. 17

commands 20
compound sentence 25
exclamations 25
fact or opinion 53
questions 34
simple sentence 25

verb .... a word or word group that tells what's happening in a **clause** or sentence 9

doing verb 9
being verb 32
saying verb 28
thinking verb 60

word family .... a group of words with the same base 69